Catapult, Inc. & Microsoft Press

Microsoft Internet Explorer 4.0 Step by Step has been created by the professional trainers and writers at Catapult, Inc., to the exacting standards you've come to expect from Microsoft Press. Together, we are pleased to present this self-paced training guide, which you can use individually or as part of a class.

Catapult, Inc. is a software training company with years of experience in PC and Macintosh instruction. Catapult's exclusive Performance-Based Training system is available in Catapult training centers across North America and at customer sites. Based on the principles of adult learning, Performance-Based Training ensures that students leave the classroom with confidence and the ability to apply skills to real-world scenarios. *Microsoft Internet Explorer 4.0 for Windows Step by Step* incorporates Catapult's training expertise to ensure that you'll receive the maximum return on your training time. You'll focus on the skills that can increase your productivity the most while working at your own pace and convenience.

Microsoft Press is the book publishing division of Microsoft Corporation. The leading publisher of information about Microsoft products and services, Microsoft Press is dedicated to providing the highest quality computer books and multimedia training and reference tools that make using Microsoft software easier, more enjoyable, and more productive.

Microsoft®
INTERNET
EXPLORER 4
Step by Step

Other titles in the *Step by Step* series:

Microsoft Access 97 Step by Step
Microsoft Excel 97 Step by Step
Microsoft Excel 97 Step by Step, Advanced Topics
Microsoft Front Page 97 Step by Step
Microsoft Office 97 Integration Step by Step
Microsoft Outlook 97 Step by Step
Microsoft PowerPoint 97 Step by Step
Microsoft Team Manager 97 Step by Step
Microsoft Windows 95 Step by Step
Microsoft Windows NT Workstation version 4.0 Step by Step
Microsoft Word 97 Step by Step
Microsoft Word 97 Step by Step, Advanced Topics

Step by Step books are also available for the Microsoft Office 95 programs.

^{Microsoft®}
INTERNET EXPLORER 4
Step by Step

Catapult

Microsoft Press

PUBLISHED BY
Microsoft Press
A Division of Microsoft Corporation
One Microsoft Way
Redmond, Washington 98052-6399

Copyright © 1997 by Catapult, Inc.

Library of Congress Cataloging-in-Publication Data
Microsoft Internet Explorer 4 Step by Step / Catapult, Inc.
    p.   cm.
    Includes index.
    ISBN 1-57231-514-8
    1. Microsoft Internet Explorer.   2. Internet (Computer network)
3. World Wide Web (Information retrieval system)   I. Catapult, Inc.
TK5105.883.M53M53   1997
005.7'13769--dc21   97-31137
                                            CIP

Printed and bound in the United States of America.

1 2 3 4 5 6 7 8 9 WCWC 2 1 0 9 8 7

Distributed to the book trade in Canada by Macmillan of Canada, a division of Canada Publishing Corporation.

A CIP catalogue record for this book is available from the British Library.

Microsoft Press books are available through booksellers and distributors worldwide. For further information about international editions, contact your local Microsoft Corporation office, or contact Microsoft Press International directly at fax (425) 936-7329. Visit our Web site at mspress.microsoft.com.

FrontPage, Microsoft, Microsoft Press, Windows, and Windows NT are registered trademarks and Active Desktop, MSN, NetMeeting, NetShow, and Outlook are trademarks of Microsoft Corporation.

Other product and company names mentioned herein may be the trademarks of their respective owners.

Companies, names, and/or data used in screens and sample output are fictitious unless otherwise noted.

For Catapult, Inc.
Lead Project Editor: Cynthia Slotvig
Project Editor: Michelle Fredette
Production Manager: Lori Kenyon
Production/Layout Editor: Carolyn Thornley
Writer: Kathy Warfel
Technical Editor: Marie Rosemund
Indexer: Julie Kawabata

For Microsoft Press
Acquisitions Editor: Susanne M. Freet
Project Editor: Laura Sackerman

Table of Contents

Table of Contents

*Quick*Look Guide

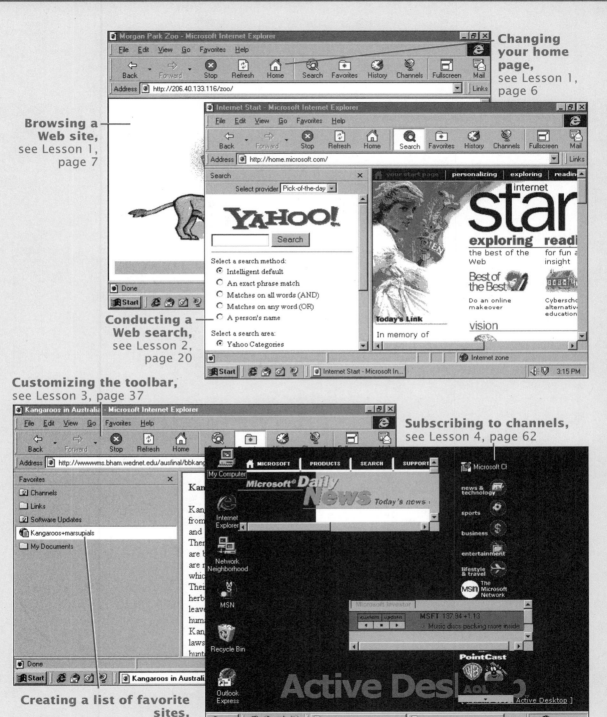

Changing your home page, see Lesson 1, page 6

Browsing a Web site, see Lesson 1, page 7

Conducting a Web search, see Lesson 2, page 20

Customizing the toolbar, see Lesson 3, page 37

Subscribing to channels, see Lesson 4, page 62

Creating a list of favorite sites, see Lesson 2, page 26

Composing and responding to e-mail messages, see Lesson 6, pages 105 and 114

Creating a Web page, see Lesson 5, page 89

Creating a signature file, see Lesson 6, page 108

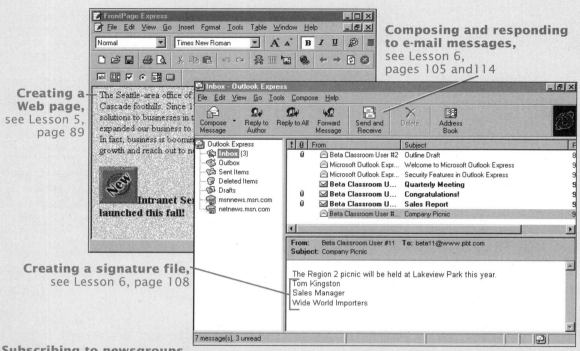

Subscribing to newsgroups, see Lesson 7, page 126

Chatting with NetMeeting, see Lesson 8, page 149

Reading newsgroup messages, see Lesson 7, page 129

Finding Your Best Starting Point

Microsoft Internet Explorer 4 is a powerful Web browser program. With *Microsoft Internet Explorer 4 Step by Step*, you'll quickly and easily learn how to use Internet Explorer to browse the World Wide Web, add Web pages to your Desktop, and communicate with people around the world on the Internet.

 IMPORTANT This book is designed for use with Internet Explorer 4 for the Windows 95 and Windows NT version 4.0 operating systems. If you already have Internet Explorer on your system, and you are not going to install it from the CD-ROM that accompanies this book, you can find out what version of Internet Explorer you're running by clicking the Help menu at the top of the Internet Explorer screen, and then clicking About Internet Explorer. If your software is not compatible with this book, a Step by Step book for your software is probably available. Many of the Step by Step titles are listed on the second page of this book. If the book you want isn't listed, please visit our World Wide Web site at http://mspress.microsoft.com or call 1-800-MSPRESS for more information.

Finding Your Best Starting Point in This Book

This book is designed for readers learning Internet Explorer 4 for the first time and for more experienced readers who want to learn and use the new features in Internet Explorer 4. Use the following table to find your best starting point in this book.

If you are	Follow these steps
New... to computers to graphical (as opposed to text-only) computer programs to Windows 95 or Windows NT	**1** Install Internet Explorer 4 and the practice files as described in "Using the Microsoft Internet Explorer 4 Step by Step CD-ROM." **2** Become acquainted with the Windows 95 or Windows NT operating system and how to use the online Help system by working through the article "If You Are New to Windows 95 or Windows NT," which is on the Microsoft Internet Explorer 4 Steb by Step CD-ROM in the file Newtowin.htm. **3** Learn basic skills for using Internet Explorer by working sequentially through Lessons 1 through 3. Then, you can work through Lessons 4 through 8 in any order.

If you are	Follow these steps
Switching... from Netscape Navigator from Mosaic	**1** Install Internet Explorer 4 and the practice files as described in "Using the Microsoft Internet Explorer 4 Step by Step CD-ROM." **2** Learn basic skills for using Internet Explorer by working sequentially through Lessons 1 through 3. Then, you can work through Lessons 4 through 8 in any order.

If you are	Follow these steps
Upgrading... from Internet Explorer 3.0 or earlier	**1** Learn about the new features in this version of the program that are covered in this book by reading through "New Features in Internet Explorer 4." **2** Install Internet Explorer 4 and the practice files as described in "Using the Microsoft Internet Explorer 4 Step by Step CD-ROM." **3** Complete the lessons that cover the topics you need. You can use the table of contents and the *Quick*Look Guide to locate information about general topics. You can use the index to find information about a specific topic or a feature from a previous version of Internet Explorer.

If you are	Follow these steps
Referencing... this book after working through the lessons	**1** Use the index to locate information about specific topics, and use the table of contents and the *Quick*Look Guide to locate information about general topics.
	2 Read the Lesson Summary at the end of each lesson for a brief review of the major tasks in the lesson. The Lesson Summary topics are listed in the same order as they are presented in the lesson.

New Features in Internet Explorer 4

The following table lists the major new features in Internet Explorer 4 that are covered in this book. The table shows the lesson in which you can learn how to use each feature. You can also use the index to find specific information about a feature or a task.

To learn how to	See
View pages on your History list	Lesson 3
Display items from the Web on the Active Desktop	Lesson 4
Add sites to your Channel Bar	Lesson 4
Subscribe to Web pages	Lesson 4
Read Web pages offline	Lesson 4
Send and receive e-mail in Outlook Express	Lesson 6
Read and post newsgroup messages in Outlook Express	Lesson 7
Conduct online meetings	Lesson 8

Corrections, Comments, and Help

Every effort has been made to ensure the accuracy of this book and the contents of the practice files on the accompanying CD-ROM. Microsoft Press provides corrections and additional content for its books through the World Wide Web at

http://mspress.microsoft.com/mspress/support

If you have comments, questions, or ideas regarding this book or the practice files CD-ROM, please send them to us.

Send e-mail to:

mspinput@microsoft.com

Or send postal mail to:

Microsoft Press

Attn: Step by Step Series Editor

One Microsoft Way

Redmond, WA 98052-6399

Please note that support for the Internet Explorer 4 software product itself is not offered through the above addresses. For help using Internet Explorer 4, you can call Microsoft Internet Explorer Technical Support at (425) 635-7123 on weekdays between 6 a.m. and 6 p.m. Pacific time.

Visit Our World Wide Web Site

We invite you to visit the Microsoft Press World Wide Web site. You can visit us at the following location:

http://mspress.microsoft.com

You'll find descriptions for all of our books, information about ordering titles, notice of special features and events, additional content for Microsoft Press books, and much more.

You can also find out the latest in software developments and news from Microsoft Corporation by visiting the following World Wide Web site:

http://www.microsoft.com

We look forward to your visit on the Web!

Using the Microsoft Internet Explorer 4 Step by Step CD-ROM

The CD-ROM inside the back cover of this book contains practice files that you'll use as you do the exercises in the book. For example, when you're learning how to edit a Web page, you'll open one of the practice files—the Western.htm Web page—and then add a picture and some text to the page. By using the practice files, you won't waste time creating the samples used in the lessons—instead, you can concentrate on learning how to use Internet Explorer, Outlook Express, FrontPage Express, and NetMeeting. With the files and the step-by-step instructions in the lessons, you'll also learn by doing, which is an easy and effective way to acquire and remember new skills.

The CD-ROM also contains the Starter Kit you need to install Internet Explorer 4, a Glossary file that contains definitions of all of the terms printed in italics in this book, links to the book's Web Picks, and the Newtowin.htm file which you should read if you are new to Windows 95 or Windows NT. In addition, the CD-ROM contains Appendix A, "Establishing Your Internet Connection," and Appendix B, "Using Microsoft Chat," as well as audiovisual files that demonstrate how to perform some of the more complicated tasks in this book.

IMPORTANT Before you break the seal on the practice CD-ROM package, be sure that this book matches your version of the software. This book is designed for use with Microsoft Internet Explorer 4 for the Windows 95 and Windows NT version 4.0 operating systems. To find out what software you're running, you can check the product package or you can start the software, and then on the Help menu at the top of the screen, click About Microsoft Internet Explorer 4. If your program is not compatible with this book, a Step by Step book matching your software is probably available. Many of the Step by Step titles are listed on the second page of this book. If the book you want isn't listed, please visit our World Wide Web site at http://mspress.microsoft.com or call 1-800-MSPRESS for more information.

Install the practice files on your computer

Follow these steps to install the practice files on your computer's hard disk so you can use them with the exercises in this book.

 NOTE If you are new to Windows 95 or Windows NT, you might want to work through "If You Are New to Windows 95 or Windows NT," which is on the CD-ROM in the file Newtowin.htm before installing the practice files. To open the Newtowin.htm file, insert the CD-ROM and click the file.

You will also be prompted for a username and password when starting Windows 95 if your computer is configured for user profiles.

Close

1 If your computer isn't on, turn it on now.

2 If you're using Windows NT, press CTRL+ALT+DEL to display a dialog box asking for your username and password. If you are using Windows 95, you will see this dialog box if your computer is connected to a network. If you don't know your username or password, contact your system administrator for assistance.

3 Type your username and password in the appropriate boxes, and then click OK. If you see the Welcome dialog box, click the Close button.

4 Remove the CD-ROM from the package inside the back cover of this book.

5 Insert the CD-ROM in your CD-ROM drive.

6 On the taskbar at the bottom of your screen, click the Start button.

The Start menu opens.

7 On the Start menu, click Run.

Click Start...⎯⎯⎯ ...and then click Run.

The Run dialog box appears.

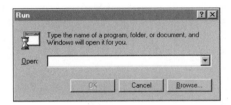

8 In the Open box, type **d:\setup** (or replace the letter "d" with the appropriate CD-ROM drive letter). Don't add spaces as you type.

9 Click OK, and then follow the directions on the screen.

The Setup program window appears with recommended options preselected for you. For best results in using the practice files with this book, accept these preselected settings.

10 When the files have been installed, remove the CD-ROM from your drive and replace it in the package inside the back cover of the book.

A folder called Internet Explorer 4 SBS Practice has been created on your hard disk, and the practice files have been put in that folder.

Microsoft
Press
Welcome

NOTE In addition to installing the practice files, the Setup program creates a shortcut on your Desktop. You can click the Microsoft Press Welcome shortcut to visit the Microsoft Press Web site. You can also connect to this Web site directly at http://mspress.microsoft.com

Install The Microsoft Network

See "Signing Up with the Microsoft Network (MSN)" in Appendix A on the CD-ROM for more information.

The companion CD also contains the client software for The Microsoft Network (MSN), Microsoft's Internet online service. Install MSN now to get **one month free** unlimited access to MSN and the Internet. To try MSN, follow these steps:

1 On the taskbar at the bottom of your screen, click the Start button, and then click Run.

2 Type **d:\msn\msnstart.exe** (or, if your CD-ROM drive uses a drive letter other than "d," substitute the correct drive letter).

3 Click OK, and then follow the directions on the screen to install MSN.

4 When prompted for a registration number, enter **9126**

For help with MSN, call Technical Support at (425) 635-7019 (English) or (425) 635-7020 (French) in the U.S. or Canada.

Using the Practice Files

Each lesson in this book explains when and how to use any practice files for that lesson. When it's time to use a practice file, the book will list instructions on how to open the file. Lessons 1-4 do not require practice files. All of the lessons are built around scenarios that simulate a real work environment, so you can easily apply the skills you learn to your own work. For example, in Part 1, you take on the roles of different employees at the Morgan Park Zoo. In Part 2, you're a computer consultant at Ferguson and Bardell, and in Part 3, you perform multiple jobs at the importing firm Wide World Importers.

The screen illustrations in this book might look different from what you see on your computer, depending on how your computer is set up. Because the Internet is such a dynamic environment, the Morgan Park Zoo site you use in Part 1 of this book has been published on the Web as a companion to this book to reduce inconsistencies. The Web site will not change, so you should be able to learn the skills taught with little variance from the steps.

Here's a list of the files included on the CD-ROM:

File name	Description
Lesson 5	
Western.htm	A Web page describing the Western Division office of the Ferguson and Bardell company.
Back.gif	The background graphic used on the Western Division Web page.
Eagle.jpg	The eagle picture used on the Western Division Web page.

File name	Description
New.jpg	The New button you add to the Western Division Web page.
Review & Practice 2	
Profiles.htm	The Employee Profiles Web page for the Ferguson and Bardell company.
Back.gif	The background graphic used on the Employee Profiles Web page.
Divider.jpg	The divider line used on the Employee Profiles Web page.
Lesson 6	
Sales.htm	The Monthly Sales Report file you attach to an e-mail message.
World.gif	The globe graphic used on the Monthly Sales Report.
Lesson 8	
Policy.txt	The agenda for the policy meeting you conduct using NetMeeting.
Pers.htm	The Online Personnel Office page you share with a collaborator in NetMeeting.
World.gif	The globe graphic used on the Online Personnel Office page.
Bullet.gif	The bullet graphic used on the Online Personnel Office page.
Additional Content	
Setup	Internet Explorer 4. Full installation includes Internet Explorer, FrontPage Express, Outlook Express, NetMeeting, NetShow, Web Publishing Wizard, and Microsoft Chat.
Glossary.htm	Definitions of the important terms used in this book.
Newtowin.htm	An introduction to the basics of Windows 95, Windows NT, the mouse, and online Help.
Appendix A	"Establishing Your Internet Connection" covers setting up connections to the Microsoft Network and Internet Explorer 4, and setting up mail and news accounts.

File name	Description
Appendix B	"Using Microsoft Chat" covers joining conversations with chat participants.
Web Picks	Shortcuts to the Web pages referred to in the Web Pick notes throughout the book.
AVI Files	Files that demonstrate how to perform some of the more complicated tasks in this book.

Use the Audiovisual Files

Throughout this book, you will see icons for audiovisual files for particular exercises. Use the following steps to run the audiovisual files.

1 Insert the CD-ROM in your CD-ROM drive.

2 On the taskbar, click Start, point to Programs, and then click Windows Explorer.

If you are using Windows NT, click Windows NT Explorer.

3 In the All Folders area, click Drive D (or the appropriate CD-ROM drive letter).

The contents of the CD-ROM are displayed.

4 In the Contents area, double-click the AVI Files folder.

The contents of the AVI Files folder are displayed.

5 Double-click the audiovisual file you need.

Microsoft Camcorder runs the video of the exercise. After the video is finished, Camcorder closes and you return to Windows Explorer.

6 Close Windows Explorer, and return to the exercise in the book.

Uninstall the Practice Files

Use the following steps when you want to delete the shortcut added to your Desktop and the practice files added to your hard disk by the Step by Step Setup program.

1 Click Start, point to Programs, and then click Windows Explorer.

If you are using Windows NT, click Windows NT Explorer.

2 In the All Folders area, scroll up and click Desktop.

The contents of your Desktop are displayed.

3 Click the Microsoft Press Welcome shortcut icon, and press DELETE.

If you are prompted to confirm the deletion, click Yes. The Microsoft Press Welcome shortcut icon is removed from your computer.

4 In the All Folders area, click Drive C.

The contents of your hard disk are displayed. If you installed your practice files on a drive other than Drive C, view the contents of that drive.

5 Click the Internet Explorer 4 SBS Practice folder, and then press DELETE.

If you are prompted to confirm the deletion, click Yes. The practice files are removed from your computer.

6 In the Contents area, double-click the Windows folder, and then double-click the Favorites folder.

7 Click the Internet Explorer 4 SBS Practice shortcut icon, and then press DELETE.

If you are prompted to confirm the deletion, click Yes. All practice files installed on your computer are now deleted.

Need Help with the Practice Files?

Every effort has been made to ensure the accuracy of this book and the contents of the practice files CD-ROM. If you do run into a problem, Microsoft Press provides corrections for its books through the World Wide Web at

http://mspress.microsoft.com/mspress/support

We also invite you to visit our main Web page at

http://mspress.microsoft.com

You'll find descriptions for all of our books, information about ordering titles, notices of special features and events, additional content for Microsoft Press books, and much more.

Conventions and Features Used in This Book

You can save time when you use this book by understanding, before you start the lessons, how instructions, keys to press, and so on are shown in the book. Please take a moment to read the following list, which also points out helpful features of the book that you might want to use.

 NOTE If you are unfamiliar with Windows 95, Windows NT, or mouse terminology, see the article, "If You Are New to Windows 95 or Windows NT," which is on the Microsoft Internet Explorer 4 Step by Step CD-ROM in the file Newtowin.htm. Click the Newtowin.htm file to open the file.

Conventions

- Hands-on exercises for you to follow are given in numbered lists of steps (1, 2, and so on). An arrowhead bullet (➤) indicates an exercise that has only one step.

- Text that you are to type appears in **bold**.

- A plus sign (+) between two key names means that you must press those keys at the same. For example, "Press ALT+TAB" means that you hold down the ALT key while you press TAB.

The following icons identify the different types of supplementary material:

Note labeled	Alerts you to
Note	Additional information for a step.
Tip	Suggested additional methods for a step or helpful hints.
Important	Essential information that you should check before continuing with the lesson.
Demonstration	Skills that are demonstrated in audiovisual files available on the Microsoft Internet Explorer 4 Step by Step CD-COM.
Web Pick	Information about interesting World Wide Web Sites.

Other Features of This Book

- You can build on what you learned in a lesson by trying the optional "One Step Further" exercise at the end of each lesson.
- You can get a quick reminder of how to do the tasks you learned by reading the Lesson Summary at the end of each lesson.
- You can quickly determine what online Help topics are available by referring to the Help topics listed at the end of each lesson. The Help system provides an online reference to Microsoft Internet Explorer. To learn more about online Help, see the article, "If You Are New to Windows 95 or Windows NT," on the Microsoft Internet Explorer 4 Step by Step CD-ROM in the Newtowin.htm file. Click the Newtowin.htm file to open the file.
- You can practice major skills by working through the Review & Practice sections at the end of each part.
- You can use the Glossary on the Microsoft Internet Explorer 4 Step by Step CD-ROM to look up definitions of Internet terms. Double-click the Glossary.htm file to open the Glossary.
- You can view audiovisual demonstrations of more complicated tasks in Internet Explorer from the CD-ROM that came with this book. To learn how to access these demonstrations see "Using the Microsoft Internet Explorer 4 Step by Step CD-ROM."

Part

1

Exploring the Internet

Browsing the World Wide Web

In this lesson you will learn how to:

**Estimated time
30 min.**

- Start Internet Explorer and connect to the Internet.
- Specify a different home page.
- Browse through a World Wide Web site.
- Create a shortcut to a Web page.
- Personalize your own start page.
- Set up a content ratings guide.

The *Internet* is one of the most vibrant and revolutionary forms of communication we have today. Connecting people of all ages from around the world, the Internet gives you access to a wealth of information and enables you to conduct everything from business transactions to poetry readings, online debates and friendly correspondence via your computer. During a typical day, you can review product information for that new office equipment you need to buy, collect sales figures from your worldwide team via e-mail, and send out a call for research papers to zoology newsgroups. You can also obtain directions to a business meeting using an online map, check current news headlines on MSNBC, help your child research a science report on bats, and visit culinary sites to decide what to make for dinner.

The Internet is made up of networks of computers that communicate and exchange information with each other. The fastest-growing part of the Internet is the *World Wide Web,* which contains information presented in text, graphic, video, and audio formats. World Wide Web sites are formatted in *Hypertext Markup Language* (HTML) which, among other things, supports *links* to other sites, so you can move easily from one page to another. To view Web pages, you need a *browser* program, like Microsoft Internet Explorer, to interpret the HTML codes and display the information on your screen.

With Internet Explorer, you can locate information quickly and manage the abundance of information available on the Web. Internet Explorer integrates the browser with your PC. This means that Internet options have been added to the Desktop so you can access information on the Web as easily as you access information on your PC.

Setting the Scene

The exercises in this book present different situations that show you how to use the Internet for business and personal use. As a newly hired tour leader at the Morgan Park Zoo, you want to familiarize yourself with the animals and exhibits at the zoo. You have heard that the zoo has an excellent Web site and you decide to use the Internet to get acquainted with your new job. In subsequent lessons, you'll take on the roles of different employees at the Morgan Park Zoo to learn how to browse the Web, search for information on the Web, and customize your Internet Explorer environment.

Later in the book, acting as a computer consultant, you'll learn how to add Web pages to your Desktop, subscribe to Web sites, and save, edit, and print a Web page. Finally, in three different capacities at an import firm, you'll use the Internet to manage a sales team, gather information from newsgroups, and conduct a meeting.

Starting Microsoft Internet Explorer

To connect to the Internet, you need a *network connection* or a *dial-up connection*. A network connection is used primarily by businesses with direct access to the Internet. A dial-up connection is used by PC owners with a modem and a phone line to connect to the Internet.

When you first connect to Internet Explorer, a message is displayed asking if you want to use the new Internet Explorer features. We recommend that you select the Web-style option, including the single-click feature. You can change this setting at any time by clicking the Start button, and under Setting, clicking Folders and Icons. On the General tab, select the desired settings.

 NOTE For more information about connecting to the Internet with your PC and a modem, see Appendix A, "Establishing Your Internet Connection" on the CD-ROM. For more information about network connections, contact your network administrator.

Start Internet Explorer

In this exercise, you start Internet Explorer so you can begin exploring the Web.

IMPORTANT To complete this lesson, you must have a dial-up connection to an Internet Service Provider or a network connection to the Internet. You must also have Internet Explorer 4 installed with Active Desktop enabled. You can add the Active Desktop during installation by choosing to install the Windows Desktop Update. For more information on installing Internet Explorer, see Appendix A, "Establishing Your Internet Connection."

Internet Explorer

With the Windows Desktop Update feature of Internet Explorer enabled, you can click to select Desktop items or folders.

1 On the Desktop, click The Internet Explorer icon.

You can also click the Launch Internet Explorer Browser icon on the taskbar to start Internet Explorer.

The Internet Explorer window opens, and if you have selected MSN as your service provider, The Microsoft Network Sign In dialog box appears. If you have not installed The Microsoft Network, a dialog box asking if you want to install it appears.

NOTE For best results, install your Internet Service Provider before installing Internet Explorer 4. For the purposes of this book, it is assumed that you have chosen The Microsoft Network as your Internet Service Provider. If you have chosen another service provider and need help with installation, please see Appendix A, "Establishing your Internet Connection" on the CD-ROM.

2 If necessary, in the Member ID box, type your Member ID.

If you installed MSN earlier, your Member ID is displayed in the Member ID box.

3 In the Password box, type your password.

If you don't want to type your password every time you connect to The Microsoft Network, select the Remember My Password check box. But remember, if you choose this option, anyone using MSN on your computer has access to your MSN account.

As the page loads on your screen, the user feedback area of the Status bar shows how many items for the page remain to be loaded.

4 Click Connect.

The Internet Explorer window opens, and the Internet Start page appears.

5 If the Internet Explorer window is not maximized, maximize it.

NOTE The content on the Internet Start page is updated constantly. The words and pictures you see in the articles on your screen might not match the articles in the illustration.

Standard toolbar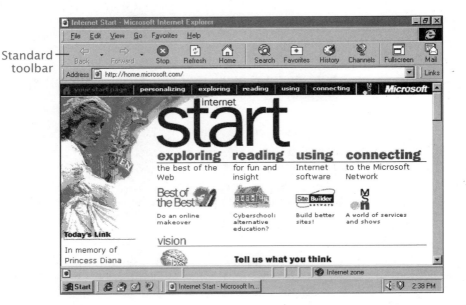

Specifying a Different Home Page

After viewing a number of sites around the Web, you might want to change your home page. Many people use their company's page or their personal Web page as their home page. In this exercise, you designate the Microsoft Home Page as your home page. After you have completed the exercises in this book, you might want to follow these steps to replace the Microsoft Home Page with a page of your choice.

1   On the View menu, click Internet Options.

2   Be sure that the General tab is selected.

3   In the Home Page area, be sure that http://home.microsoft.com is displayed in the Address box.

    If the Microsoft Home Page address is not displayed in the Address box, type http://home.microsoft.com/

4 Click OK.

5 To be sure that you typed the correct address, on the Standard toolbar, click Home.

The Microsoft Home Page should be displayed. If it is not, go through the steps again and check the address.

Browsing a Web Site

Now that your start page is set, you can explore the Web and visit sites not linked to your start page.

For a demon-stration of how to browse a site, refer to p.xxii in the Using the Microsoft Internet Explorer 4 Step by Step CD-ROM section.

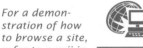

WEB PICK Want to view some top-rated Web sites? Visit http:// point.lycos.com/categories and click Top 5% to see what the folks at Lycos have selected as interesting sites.

To keep the millions of pages that make up the Web organized, each page has a unique address, or *Uniform Resource Locator* (URL), that identifies where the page is located on the Internet. The following table describes the components that make up a URL, using the Internet Explorer URL of http:// www.microsoft.com/ie/ie40/demos.htm as an example.

Example	Component	Description
http://	Service type	Tells the browser which Internet *protocol* to use to retrieve the page. All Web page URLs start with this service type.
www.microsoft.com/	Domain name	The server where the page is located.
ie/ie40/	Directory path	The path to the Web page.
demos.htm	File name	File name of the Web page.

What happens if you want to find a Web page but do not know the full URL? You can enter the service type and domain name and then follow links from there. For example, if you do not know the full URL of the Internet Explorer page, but you know that the page is at the Microsoft site, you can enter http:// www.microsoft.com and jump to different pages until you find the one that you want.

Most companies and organizations have created domain names similar to their well-known names and often you can locate them on the Web by making an educated guess.

Identifying Different Kinds of Web Addresses

Internet domain names include an identifier that designates what type of organization the name represents. For example, the ".com" at the end of www.microsoft.com indicates that it is a commercial site. There are six domain name identifiers in common use. As of the writing of this book, seven more identifiers have been proposed to handle the increased demand for domain names generated by the fast growth of the Web.

The commonly used identifiers are:

.com	Commercial businesses
.edu	Educational institutions
.gov	Government entities
.mil	Military sites
.net	Internet Service Providers
.org	A miscellaneous identifier for organizations not falling into other categories

Some Web addresses also include a two-character country code following the identifier. For example, ca is the code for Canada. You can find a complete list of country codes at http://www.ics.uci.edu/pub/websoft/wwwstat/country-codes.txt

WEB PICK Read your favorite works of classic literature at the Project Gutenberg site at http://www.promo.net/pg

Open a Web Page by using the URL

In this exercise, you go directly to the Morgan Park Zoo Web page by entering the full URL.

1 Click in the Address box.

The URL in the Address box is highlighted. If it is not, drag to select the entire URL.

The http:// service type is inserted automatically at the beginning of the URL.

2 Type **www.highway99.com/zoo** and press ENTER.

The Morgan Park Zoo home page appears. Your screen should look similar to the following illustration.

Address box

 TIP With Internet Explorer's AutoComplete feature, you can type the first few characters of a recently used URL into the Address box, and the remainder of the URL is filled in.

Using the Address Box for Other Service Types

There are other service types, besides http://, you can use in the Address box. For example, using the file:// service type allows you to see how a Web page you created will look in a browser before making it available on the Internet. Since Web pages are coded in HTML, it is a good idea to preview your page in a browser to be sure the codes give you the results you want. For example, to see your page in Internet Explorer, you would enter file://c:\myfile.htm in the Address box.

The following table describes the service types most often used on the Internet.

Service type	Is used to
file://	Open a file on a hard drive or a floppy disk in your browser.
ftp://	Copy files to or from your computer over the Internet. FTP stands for *File Transfer Protocol.*
gopher://	Access a menu-based index of information on the Internet. Gopher was named for the mascot of the University of Minnesota, where Gopher originated.
http://	Transfer hypertext pages on the World Wide Web. HTTP stands for Hypertext Transfer Protocol.
telnet://	Log on to a remote computer and use your keyboard as though you were a user on that computer.
wais://	Search a set of indexed databases to find information on the Internet. WAIS stands for Wide Area Information Server.

Browse the Morgan Park Zoo site

In this exercise, you learn how to stop loading a Web page and how to refresh a Web page as you browse the Morgan Park Zoo site.

You can also stop loading a page by pressing the ESC key or by selecting Stop on the View menu.

1   On the Morgan Park Zoo home page, scroll down, and then click Exhibits.

   The Animal Exhibits page appears.

2   On the Animal Exhibits page, click the word "Birds" or the picture of the toucan.

3   As the Birds page is loading, on the toolbar, click Stop.

   The loading process stops.

4   On the toolbar, click Refresh to resume loading the Birds page.

   The Birds page appears.

5   On the Birds page, click Primates to continue browsing the zoo pages.

   You can browse through as many pages as you want.

You can also refresh the screen by selecting Refresh on the View menu.

Select pages using the Back button and the Forward button

In this exercise, you browse backward and forward through the pages of the Morgan Park Zoo.

You will learn more about how to revisit sites in Lesson 3.

1   On the toolbar, click the Back down arrow, and then click Morgan Park Zoo.

   The Morgan Park Zoo home page appears.

2   On the toolbar, click the Forward down arrow, and then click Animals.

   The Animal Exhibits page appears.

 WEB PICK   Thinking of starting or joining an investment club? Check out http://www.better-investing.org for the National Association of Investors Corporation (NAIC) page.

Creating a Shortcut to a Page

As you browse the Web, you might find pages that you would like to return to quickly. You can create a shortcut as you are viewing a Web page. The shortcut is placed on your Desktop, and you can click the shortcut whenever you want to go to the page (you need to be connected to the Internet to load the page).

Create a shortcut

In this exercise, you create a shortcut to the Morgan Park Zoo page you are currently viewing.

➤ On the File menu, point to Send, and then click Shortcut To Desktop.

The shortcut is added to your Desktop. To view the shortcut, click the Show Desktop icon on the taskbar. Click Show Desktop again to return to Internet Explorer.

Go to your home page

In this exercise, you leave the zoo pages and go back to your home page to finish reading the page.

You can also go to your home page by selecting Home Page on the Go menu.

➤ On the toolbar, click the Home button.

The Internet Start page appears.

Personalizing Your Start Page

The Internet Start page, also referred to as your home page, contains a wide range of topics with articles gathered from different providers. You can leave the page as is, or you can create a personalized start page with content supplied by the authors you choose. Much of the content offered by Internet Explorer is provided by companies that publish business and computer magazines.

Web Terminology

As the Web has grown, a vocabulary has evolved to describe items that make up the Web. The following table defines some of the most common Web-related terms.

Word	Description
Page	The online document you see in your browser window.
Link	Text or a graphic you can click to move to a new page or to a different location on the same page. Also known as a hyperlink, hot link, hypertext link, hotspot, or jump.
Site	The collection of pages available at a location. Also used as an abbreviation for "Web site."
Content	The text, graphics, and multimedia information you view at a site.
Server	The host computer where a page is stored to make it accessible on the Web.

Select a provider for your start page

In this exercise, you select the content providers whose articles you want to use on your personalized start page.

1 On the Internet Start page, position the pointer over the Personalizing Your Start Page link.

The pointer changes to a hand to indicate the word is a link. Links on Web pages are not always underlined. If you are not sure if an item is a link, you can position the mouse pointer on it; if the pointer changes to a hand, it is a link.

2 Click the Personalizing Your Start Page link.

Personalizing
Your Start
Page link

3 On the Step 1 list, click Technology.

A list of companies that provide technology information is displayed. If Wired is not shown on your Technology list, select another provider.

4 On the Step 2 list, select the MSNBC check box and the Wired check box.

NOTE You can select as many providers as you want within each category.

5 On the Step 3 list, click Finish.

The Internet Start page is reloaded to incorporate your changes.

6 Scroll down to the Technology section.

7 Articles from the selected provider are displayed. You can click any of the links to go to the full text of the article.

Delete a provider from your start page

In this exercise, you delete one of the content providers from your start page to shorten the page and make it faster to read.

1 On the Internet Start page, click the Your Personal Choices link.
2 On the Step 1 list, click Technology.
3 On the Step 2 list, clear the Wired check box.
4 On the Step 3 list, click Finish.

The page is reloaded and the provider is deleted from the page.

If you did not select Wired in the previous exercise, clear another check box you selected.

 TIP To restore all of the original providers to the Internet Start page at one time, click the link below the Finish button.

Setting Up Your Content Ratings Guide

The Web provides an arena for the open publication of information. Content published on Web pages is left to the discretion of the content provider and the author. Internet Explorer has a content ratings feature to warn you when content on a page might be objectionable.

Enable the ratings system

In this exercise, you set up a ratings guide for your computer so you can control the type of content you access on the Internet.

1 On the View menu, click Internet Options.
2 Click the Content tab.
3 In the Content Advisor area, click Enable.

The Create Supervisor Password dialog box appears.

4 In the Password box, type the password of your choice and then press TAB.
5 In the Confirm Password box, type the same password and click OK.

The Content Advisor dialog box appears with the Ratings tab selected.

6 In the Category box, click Language.
7 Drag the slider to select the language level you want to be viewed on your PC.

The Description box shows you a longer description of each level. Your screen should look similar to the following illustration.

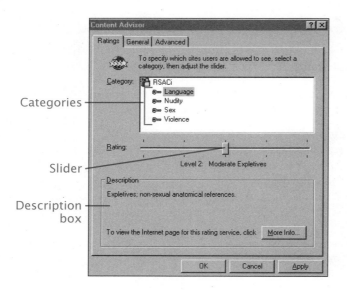

Categories

Slider

Description box

8 Repeat steps 6 and 7 for each of the remaining categories.

9 Click OK.

A message indicating that Content Advisor has been installed successfully is displayed.

10 Click OK until the Options dialog box is closed.

Turn off the ratings system

Many pages on the Web are not rated. An unrated page might bring up the ratings warning, even though the content is acceptable. In this exercise, you learn how to disable the ratings system so that you can browse the Web without receiving the ratings warning.

1 On the View menu, click Internet Options.

2 Click the Content tab.

3 In the Content Advisor area, click Disable.

4 In the Supervisor Password Required dialog box, type the password, and click OK.

5 In the Content Advisor dialog box, click OK.

6 In the Internet Options dialog box, click OK.

NOTE If you'd like to build on the skills that you learned in this lesson, you can work through the exercises in One Step Further. Otherwise, skip to "Finish the lesson."

One Step Further: Adding Your Address and Credit Card Information to Wallet

The Wallet program allows you to quickly purchase items from a Web site. Your billing addresses and credit card numbers are stored securely on your PC. When you visit sites that use the Wallet program, you can select the address and card you want to use, and make your purchases without having to re-enter your credit card information at each store.

Add your address information

As you browse different sites, you will notice that there is a lot to buy on the Web. In this exercise, you store your personal billing address and credit card number in your Internet Explorer Wallet.

1   On the View menu, click Internet Options.

2   In the Internet Options dialog box, click the Content tab.

3   In the Personal Information area, click Addresses.

4   In the Address Options dialog box, click Add.

5   In the Add A New Address dialog box, enter the appropriate information. Press TAB to move to the next field as you enter the information.

6   In the Display Name area, if the Home button is not already clicked, click it.

7   Click OK.

8   On the Address Options dialog box, click Close.

    The address information is added.

Add your payment information

1   On the Internet Options dialog box, in the Personal Information area, click Payments. In the Installing Payment Extensions dialog box, click Install.

2   In the Payment Options dialog box, click the Add button, and then select the type of card you are inputting.

3   In the License Agreement dialog box, click I Agree.

4   Click Next, and then enter the appropriate credit card information.

5   On the Credit Card Information screen, click Next.

6   On the Credit Card Billing Address screen, click Next.

7   In the Add New Address screen, enter your information, click OK, and then click Next.

A license agreement for Microsoft Wallet appears the first time you enter payment information in Wallet. You can proceed only if you accept the agreement.

8   On the Credit Card Password screen, in the Password box, enter the password you want to use, and then press TAB.

9   In the Confirm Password box, enter the password again, and then click Finish.

The payment information is added.

10   On the Payment Options dialog box, click Close.

11   On the Internet Options dialog box, click OK.

Delete the payment information

You can use this exercise if you decide to stop using this credit card to purchase items from Web sites. In this exercise, you delete the payment information.

1   On the View menu, click Internet Options.

2   Click the Content tab.

3   In the Personal Information area, click Payments.

4   In the Cards area, click the card you want to delete, and then click Delete.

5   In the Delete Credit Card dialog box, click Yes.

The payment information is deleted.

6   On the Payment Options dialog box, click Close.

 TIP   The address information is not deleted when you delete the payment information. To delete the address, in the Personal Information area, click Addresses, select the address, and then click Delete.

7   On the Internet Options dialog box, click OK.

Finish the lesson

1   To continue to the next lesson, on the toolbar, click Home.

2   If you are finished using Internet Explorer for now, on the File menu, click Close.

The Microsoft Network dialog box appears.

If you are using a network connection, skip step 3.

3   Click Yes to disconnect from The Microsoft Network.

Lesson Summary

To	Do this	Button
Start Internet Explorer	On the Desktop, click The Internet Explorer icon.	
Go to your home page	On the toolbar, click Home.	
Specify a different home page	On the View menu, click Internet Options. Select the General tab. In the Home Page area on the Address bar, type in the desired URL. Click OK.	
Open a page with its URL	On the Internet Explorer screen, click in the Address box. Type the URL.	
Stop loading a page	While the page is loading, on the toolbar, click Stop.	
Refresh a page	On the toolbar, click Refresh.	
Select pages from the Back and Forward lists	On the toolbar, click the Back down arrow. Click the item you want to see. Click the Forward down arrow. Click the item you want to see.	
Create a shortcut to a Web page	On the File menu, point to Send, and then click Shortcut To Desktop.	
Select a provider for your start page	On the Internet Start page, click Personalizing. On the Step 1 list, click a topic. On the Step 2 list, click the providers you want to select. Click Finish.	
Delete a provider from your start page	On the Internet Start page, click Personalizing. On the Step 1 list, click a topic. On the Step 2 list, clear the check box of the provider you want to delete. Click Finish.	
Set up your ratings guide	On the View menu, click Internet Options. Click the Content tab. Click Enable. Enter your password, and click OK. Click Language, drag the slider, and click OK.	

To	Do this	Button
Turn off content ratings	On the View menu, click Internet Options. Click Content, and then click Disable. Type your password, and click OK until all dialog boxes are closed.	

For online information about	On the Help menu, click Contents And Index, click the Index tab, and then type	
Browsing a Web site	browsing the Web	
Using links to move from page to page	links	
Opening a page by using a Web address	addresses, using to find Web sites	
Creating a shortcut to a Web page	shortcuts, creating on the desktop	
Screening out objectionable content	ratings	

Searching for Information

Estimated time
30 min.

In this lesson you will learn how to:

- Find information on the Internet.
- Create a list of your favorite World Wide Web sites.
- Preview thumbnail pictures of your favorite Web sites.

Searching for information on the Internet is fast and efficient with Microsoft Internet Explorer. Using the Search button, you can look for a word or topic and view the list of sites that a search produces and the pages located by your search, side-by-side, on your screen. This side-by-side display makes it easy to find the information you need.

The Internet is a great resource for information about almost every topic imaginable. When you perform a search, you should be as specific as possible. If your topic is too general, you might find thousands of matching pages. For example, if you are looking for information about parrots, you get more specific results by searching for "parrots" than by searching for "birds."

WEB PICK   Looking for the latest computer news? Stop by the Computer Network at http://www.cnet.com

---

As an employee in the Community Relations department at the Morgan Park Zoo, you have been asked to write an article for a brochure your department is creating about the animals at the zoo for a "Schools and Zoos" program.

Start Internet Explorer

In this exercise, you use the Web to search for background information on the animals to help you write the article.

If you are using a service provider other than MSN or if you have a network connection, skip step 2.

1 On the Desktop, click The Internet Explorer icon.

The Internet Explorer window opens, and if you have selected MSN as your service provider, The Microsoft Network Sign In dialog box appears. If you have not installed The Microsoft Network, a dialog box appears asking if you want to install it.

2 If necessary, in the Member ID box, type your Member ID.

3 In the Password box, type your password.

If you don't want to type your password every time you connect to The Microsoft Network, select the Remember My Password check box. But remember, if you choose this option, anyone using MSN on your computer has access to your MSN account.

The Internet Explorer window opens, and the Internet Start page appears.

4 If necessary, maximize the Internet Explorer window.

Finding Information on the Web

For a demonstration of how to search for information on the Web, refer to p.xxii in the Using the Microsoft Internet Explorer 4 Step by Step CD-ROM section.

The Internet, as we know it today, was formed in the early 1980s. At that time, there were only a few hundred sites and people who accessed the Internet, most of whom were government employees, knew where to find the information they needed. As the Internet evolved, so much information became available that methods for finding and categorizing the information had to be created.

Search engines, database applications that help you find information, are the most effective of these methods. When conducting a search, you can select one of several search engines or use the Pick Of The Day search engine selected automatically in Internet Explorer when you open the Explorer Bar using the Search button.

Search for information on the Web

In this exercise, you begin your research for the zoo brochure by searching for information about kangaroos.

You can also select Search The Web on the Go menu.

1 On the toolbar, click Search.

The Explorer Bar opens in a separate pane on your screen, and one of several search engines is displayed. Your screen should look similar to the following illustration.

Explorer Bar —

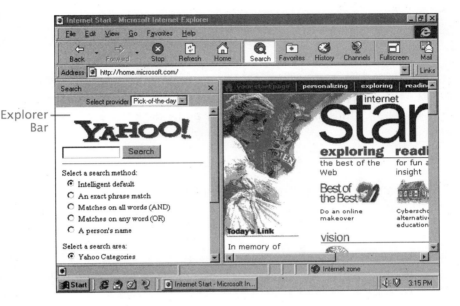

 NOTE The pane that opens when you click the Search button is known as the Explorer Bar. You can use the Explorer Bar to perform a search, create a Favorites list so you can return to your favorite Web sites easily, view your History list to get back to a previously visited Web site, or set up channels to have contents from the Internet delivered to your computer.

If the Pick Of The Day search engine is Yahoo!, skip steps 2 and 3.

2 On the Explorer Bar, click the Select Provider down arrow.

A list of search engines is displayed.

3 Select Yahoo.

4 Click in the Search box, type **kangaroos**, and then click Search.

5 In the Security Alert box, select the In The Future, Do Not Show The Warning For This Zone check box, and then click Yes.

The search results are displayed on the Explorer Bar. The Yahoo! search engine lists results by category, followed by brief summaries of each Web page.

6 Click the link to the first category.

A list of pages included in the category is displayed on the right side of your screen.

If you do not see the Kangaroo Game Preserve listed, click a different link.

7 Click Kangaroo Game Preserve.

The page appears on the right side of your screen. You can click as many links and review as many pages as you like.

TIP When the Explorer Bar is open, the Back and Forward buttons on the toolbar apply only to the information on the right side of the screen. To go back to the previous screen on the Explorer Bar, you must right-click the Explorer Bar, and then select Back on the shortcut menu.

Resize the Explorer Bar

In this exercise, you decrease the size of the Explorer Bar to gain more room for viewing the Web pages on the right side of the screen.

1 Position the pointer on the dividing line between the two panes.

The pointer changes to a two-headed arrow.

2 Drag the dividing line to the left.

The Explorer Bar narrows, giving you more room to view the Web pages.

3 Drag the dividing line back to the right so you can use the Explorer Bar for additional searches.

WEB PICK Visit the U.S. Library of Congress online at http://www.loc.gov and the National Library of Canada at http://www.nlc-bnc.ca

---

Use a different search engine

In this exercise, you select a different search engine to continue searching for information on kangaroos.

1 On the Explorer Bar, click the Select Provider down arrow.

2 Select Excite.

3 Click in the Search box, type **kangaroos**, and then click Search.

A list of Web pages is displayed on the Explorer Bar.

4 On the Explorer Bar, click a link to one of the Web pages.

The page appears on the right side of the screen.

Refining Your Search

You might need to refine your search if you find no matching Web pages, or if there are too many Web pages for you to examine.

Why Do I Get Different Results with Different Search Engines?

It would be impossible to look through the millions of pages on the Web every time you conduct a search. When you perform a search, you are accessing the search engine's database of information. The entries in the database are indexed so they can be located quickly. Programs called *crawlers* go through the database and search the indexes for information that matches the word or phrase you entered.

The databases are updated periodically with information from new or modified Web pages. The results you receive might be different from one provider to another because different pages have been examined by each database, the information has been indexed in a different way, or the databases contain different keywords.

Some providers have expanded their search capabilities beyond Web pages to allow you to search newsgroups and other parts of the Internet and the Web. Your results might differ from provider to provider if you are searching different parts of the Internet.

You can refine your search by adding more keywords or by using special operators that tell the search engines to exclude some words or to look for combinations of words. For example, the search for kangaroos yielded Web pages dealing with kangaroos, sports teams, and Kangaroo Island. To narrow the search to animals only, you can use the special operator "+" to instruct the search engine to select only Web pages that contain both "kangaroos" and "marsupials."

 NOTE Each search engine has a page that shows the rules and syntax you use to refine a search and which special operators are used by the engine. For example, in the Excite search engine, the syntax rules are located at the Search Tips link. Other search engines have similar links to pages that describe how to limit a search.

Refine the search terms

In this exercise, you refine your search to limit the results to Web pages about kangaroos and marsupials.

1 On the Explorer Bar, scroll to the top of the page.

The Excite search engine is still selected.

2 In the Search box, click to the right of the word "kangaroos."

Be sure that you do not type a space before or after the plus sign in step 3.

3 Next to kangaroos in the Search box, type **+marsupials**, and then click Search.

The search results are displayed on the Explorer Bar. The sports-related pages have been screened out, and the results show only pages relating to both "kangaroos" and "marsupials."

 NOTE The "+" sign is the special operator used by Excite. Other search engines might use a different operator or syntax. Be sure to check the Search Tips or similar link if you are using a different search engine.

4 Click one of the Web page links.

The page appears on the right side of the screen.

Using Autosearch

If you want to search for one item quickly but you do not want to see the side-by-side search results, you can enter the word or phrase you are looking for directly on the Address bar. This feature is called Autosearch in Internet Explorer. Autosearch accesses a section of the Yahoo! search provider.

To search for information using Autosearch:

1 Click in the Address bar.

2 Type **go kangaroos**, and press ENTER.

You can also type **find kangaroos** or **? kangaroos** on the Address bar to perform the search.

Finding a Word on a Page

When you are reading through text, it is helpful to be able to locate words without having to scroll through every line or paragraph of the text manually. In Internet Explorer, you can use the Find dialog box to search for a specific word on a Web page and go directly to that location.

Search for a word on a page

In this exercise, you search for the word "kangaroos" in the Web page you are viewing.

1 Scroll to the top of the Web page.

2 On the Edit menu, click Find (On This Page).

The Find dialog box appears.

NOTE You can search for words on the Web pages you are viewing but not on the Explorer Bar itself.

3 In the Find What box, type **kangaroos**.

Your screen should look similar to the following illustration.

4 Click Find Next.

The first occurrence of the word is located and highlighted.

If you cannot see the high-lighted word, it might be hidden by the dialog box. Drag the dialog box title bar until you see the highlighted word.

5 Click Find Next again.

The text scrolls down, and the next occurrence of the word is highlighted.

NOTE If you want to search the entire document, keep click-ing Find Next until you reach the bottom of the document. When you find no more occurrences of the word, a dialog box appears to notify you that the search is finished. Click OK to close the dialog box.

You can also click the Close button on the Explorer Bar window.

6 Click Cancel.

The Find dialog box closes.

Close the Explorer Bar

➤ On the toolbar, click Search.

The Explorer Bar closes, and the Web page you are viewing is expanded to the full screen.

25

WEB PICK   Need directions? Use the Interactive Atlas at http://www.mapquest.com

Creating a List of Your Favorite Web Sites

You will learn how to subscribe to your favorite sites in Lesson 4.

As you search the Web, you will find pages that you want to refer to again. You do not need to memorize or write down the URL; you can add the page to your Favorites list. When you add a page to your Favorites, you are adding a shortcut to the page, and not the content of the page, to your Favorites list.

Favorites are not limited to Web sites. You can add files stored on your PC or on your company's network to your list of Favorites. Your Favorites are shown on the Explorer Bar in Internet Explorer. To go to one of the pages, you can open your Favorites list and click the page you want to see. If you are not sure which page you want to see, you can preview thumbnail pictures of pages until you locate the one you want.

Add the current page to your list of Favorites

In this exercise, you add the page on your screen to your list of Favorites.

You can also accept the Name box as is by clicking OK.

1   On the Favorites menu, click Add To Favorites.

The Add To Favorites dialog box appears.

2   In the Name box, type **Kangaroos & Marsupials**, and click OK.

The page is added to your Favorites folder.

3   Go to a Web site of your choice and add it as a favorite.

View your list of Favorites

1   On the toolbar, click Favorites.

The Explorer Bar opens. Your screen should look similar to the following illustration.

You can also click the View menu, point to Explorer Bar, and then click Favorites.

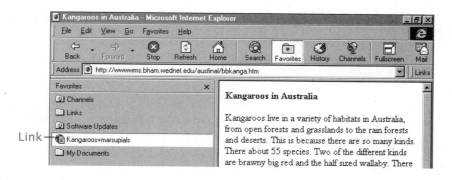

Link

2 On the Explorer Bar, click the Links folder.

The folder expands to show the sites included in the folder. The Links folder is supplied with Internet Explorer.

You can also select the Favorites menu, point to Links, and then click Best of the Web.

3 Click Best of the Web.

The Best of the Web page at the Microsoft Web site appears.

4 Click the Links folder again.

The folder collapses.

5 On the Explorer Bar, click Kangaroos & Marsupials to return to that page.

Close the Explorer Bar

You can also click the Close button on the Explorer Bar window.

➤ On the toolbar, click Favorites.

The Explorer Bar closes, and the Web page expands to fill the screen.

 WEB PICK   Libraries on the Internet never close! Research articles at the "Virtual Reference Desk" at http://thorplus.lib.purdue.edu/reference/ or browse the Internet Public Library at http://www.ipl.org

---

Organizing Your Favorites

Subfolders and links are supplied with Internet Explorer in your Favorites list. You can also create your own subfolders and organize your Favorites list just as you would organize your work files on your computer.

Create a new folder

In this exercise, you create a folder for the Schools and Zoos brochure.

1 On the Favorites menu, click Organize Favorites.

The Organize Favorites dialog box appears.

2 Click the Create New Folder button.

The new folder is added to the screen with the name New Folder highlighted.

Create New Folder

3 Type **Schools and Zoos**, and press ENTER.

A new folder called Schools And Zoos is created.

4 Click any blank space in the Organize Favorites dialog box.

The Schools And Zoos folder is no longer highlighted.

Move your favorites into a new folder

In this exercise, you move the Kangaroos & Marsupials link to the folder you just created.

1 In the Organize Favorites dialog box, click Kangaroos & Marsupials.

You can also drag the Kangaroos & Marsupials link to the Schools And Zoos folder.

2 In the Organize area, click Move.

The Browse For Folder dialog box appears.

3 Click Schools And Zoos, and click OK.

The link is moved, and the Browse For Folder dialog box closes.

4 In the Organize Favorites dialog box, click Close.

5 On the toolbar, click the Favorites button.

The Explorer Bar opens, and the Favorites list is displayed.

6 On the Explorer Bar, click Schools And Zoos.

The folder expands, and the Kangaroos & Marsupials link is displayed.

 WEB PICK   Like to calculate anything and everything? The site at http://www-sci.lib.uci.edu/HSG/RefCalculators.html has more than 4,000 calculators you can use online.

Previewing Your Favorites in Thumbnail View

You can also preview files stored on your PC or on your company's network in Thumbnail View.

The names you assign to the items on your Favorites list help you identify the Web page the link represents. If you are looking for a page among your favorites and the names do not help you locate it, you can preview thumbnail snapshots of the first page of each Web site stored in the folder. These snapshots can help you quickly locate the page you want.

Set up Thumbnail View

In this exercise, you enable Thumbnail View for the Schools and Zoos folder.

1 On the Favorites menu, click Organize Favorites.

2 Right-click the Schools and Zoos folder.

3 On the shortcut menu, click Properties.

The Schools and Zoos Properties dialog box appears.

4 Select the Enable Thumbnail View check box, and click OK.

The Schools and Zoos Properties dialog box closes.

> **NOTE**   You must select the Enable Thumbnail View check box on each folder that you want to preview in Thumbnail View. Folders remain enabled unless you clear the Enable Thumbnail View check box.

5   On the Organize Favorites dialog box, click Close.

Preview thumbnail pictures of your favorite pages

In this exercise, you look at the thumbnail pictures in the Schools and Zoos folder.

1   On the Favorites menu, click Organize Favorites.

The Organize Favorites dialog box appears.

2   Click the Schools and Zoos folder.

The contents of the folder are displayed.

3   Right-click any blank space on the Organize Favorites dialog box.

A shortcut menu is displayed.

4   On the shortcut menu, point to View, and then click Thumbnails.

A thumbnail view of the page is displayed. Your screen should look similar to the following illustration.

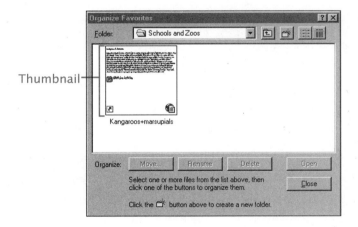

Thumbnail

5   On the Organize Favorites dialog box, click Close, and then click Home.

> **NOTE**   If you'd like to build on the skills that you learned in this lesson, you can work through the exercises in One Step Further. Otherwise, skip to "Finish the lesson."

One Step Further: Accessing Your Favorites from the Desktop

As you're writing your article on the "Schools and Zoos" program, you find a perfect spot to insert a quote about the kangaroo population in Australia. You remember seeing that information somewhere on the Internet but can't remember where. Luckily, you've added all of the kangaroo pages to your Favorites list. You can access the pages quickly using the Favorites menu on the Desktop.

When you use the Favorites menu on the Desktop, the Internet Explorer window opens automatically, and the page you've selected is displayed.

Access your Favorites from the Desktop

In this exercise, you go to a page on your Favorites list from the Desktop.

1   On the taskbar, click the Start button.

2   On the Start menu, point to Favorites.

    Your Favorites folders are displayed.

3   On the list of Favorites folders, point to Schools and Zoos.

    A list of the pages stored in the Schools and Zoos folder is displayed.

4   On the list of pages in the Schools and Zoos folder, click the first page.

    The page is displayed in the Internet Explorer window.

 TIP   When you are working in a program other than Internet Explorer, using the Favorites menu on the Desktop is the fastest way to access a Favorites page.

Finish the lesson

Follow these steps to delete the Schools and Zoos folder and finish the lesson.

If you want to keep the Schools and Zoos folder, skip steps 1 through 3.

1   On the Favorites menu, click Organize Favorites.

2   Click the Schools and Zoos folder, and then click Delete.

3   In the Confirm Folder Delete dialog box, click Yes.

4   On the Organize Favorites dialog box, click Close.

5   To continue to the next lesson, on the toolbar, click Home.

6   If you are finished using Internet Explorer for now, on the File menu, click Close.

If you are using a network connection, skip steps 7 and 8.

7   On the taskbar, right-click the Connection icon.

8   Click Sign Out.

Lesson Summary

To	Do this	Button
Search the Web	On the toolbar, click Search. On the Explorer Bar, click the Service Provider down arrow, and then select a provider. Type the word(s) you want to search for in the Search box, and then click Search.	
Resize the Explorer Bar	Drag the divider line to the left or right.	
Refine your search	On the Explorer Bar, use a more specific word or a special operator in the Search box.	
Find a word on a page	On the Edit menu, click Find (On This Page). Type the word you want to locate, and then click Find Next. When you are finished, click Cancel.	
Close the Explorer Bar	On the toolbar, click the active button.	
Add the current page to Favorites	On the Favorites menu, click Add To Favorites. Type the name you want to assign to the item, and click OK.	
View your list of Favorites	On the toolbar, click Favorites.	
Create a new folder	On the Favorites menu, click Organize Favorites. Click the Create New Folder button. Type the folder name, and press ENTER.	
Move a favorite item to a new folder	On the Favorites menu, click Organize Favorites. Click the item you want to move, and click Move.	
Set up Thumbnail View	On the Favorites menu, click Organize Favorites. Right-click the folder of your choice, and then click Properties. Click Enable Thumbnail View, and click OK.	

31

To	Do this
Preview thumbnail pictures	On the Favorites menu, click Organize Favorites. Click the folder of your choice. Right-click any blank space. On the shortcut menu, point to View, and then click Thumbnails.

For online information about	On the Help menu, click Contents And Index, click the Index tab, and then type
Searching for information on the Web	searching
Searching for a word on a Web page	searching
Using the Explorer Bar	search button
Creating a list of Favorites	favorite Web sites
Organizing Favorites	favorite Web sites

Getting Comfortable in Internet Explorer

Estimated time
25 min.

In this lesson you will learn how to:

■ Customize the Microsoft Internet Explorer screen.

■ View entries in the History folder and specify the number of days to keep pages in history.

■ Add sites to security zones.

With the abundance and variety of information available on the World Wide Web, you can spend hours reading interesting Web pages. Therefore, it's important for you to be comfortable with your online environment. You can customize Internet Explorer so the options you use the most are easy to locate and function comfortably for you.

With one feature, you can change the appearance of Web pages on your screen and experiment with different formats. For example, you can display the print in a larger size to make it easier to read, change link colors to match your favorite colors, or remove the toolbars to devote the full screen to the Web page contents.

As you travel the Web, you accumulate a history list of the pages you have visited. You can customize your History list by selecting the number of days of history you want to view. In addition, you can assign Web sites to the security zones supplied with Internet Explorer to ensure safe travels on the Web.

WEB PICK Find the answers to your medical questions at the Mayo Clinic at http://www.mayo.ivi.com

In your role as a researcher at the Morgan Park Zoo, you find that you are using your PC many hours a day. In this exercise, you customize your Internet Explorer screen to match the settings on the PC you use at home.

Start Internet Explorer

 IMPORTANT To complete this lesson, you must have a dial-up connection to an Internet Service Provider or a network connection to the Internet. You must also have Internet Explorer 4 installed. For more information on setting up your connection and installing Internet Explorer, see Appendix A, "Establishing Your Internet Connection" on the CD-ROM.

You can also click the Launch Internet Explorer Browser icon on the taskbar.

1 On the Desktop, click The Internet Explorer icon.

The Internet Explorer window opens. The Microsoft Network Sign In dialog box appears, and your Member ID is displayed in the Member ID box.

If you are using a service provider other than MSN, or if you have a network connection, skip steps 2 and 3.

2 In the Password box, type your password.

If you do not want to type your password every time you connect to The Microsoft Network, select the Remember My Password check box. But remember, if you choose this option, anyone using MSN on your computer has access to your MSN account.

3 If necessary, maximize the Internet Explorer window.

Customizing the Internet Explorer Screen

When you view a Web page, you can change the text size and the link colors to suit your personal preferences. Some people like smaller print so they can see more information on one screen, while others prefer larger print so they can read information more easily.

You can customize your screen to display links in colors you choose. This is convenient if you have trouble viewing certain colors or prefer using your favorite colors. Links appear in one color before you visit them and in a different color after you visit them to help you track your progress through a Web site.

NOTE The changes you make are stored in Internet Explorer and apply only to your screen. The changes do not affect the Web pages on the Internet.

Reset the font size

In this exercise, you increase the *font*, or type style, size on one of the pages at the Morgan Park Zoo Web site.

Increasing or decreasing the font size does not affect the size of the graphics.

1 In the Address box, type http://www.highway99.com/zoo/ and press ENTER.

2 At the bottom of the page, click the Visitor Info button.

The Visitor Information page appears.

3 On the View menu, point to Fonts.

The Font menu is displayed.

4 On the Font menu, click Largest.

The size of the text increases.

How Can the Default Font Be Changed?

The default font in Internet Explorer is Times New Roman. If there is a different font you want to use, you can change the default font. On the View menu, click Options, and then click the Fonts button. In the Fonts dialog box, your default character set is displayed. Then, click the Proportional Font down arrow, select your desired font, and click OK. The font is added to the character set.

Select colors

In this exercise, you change the colors of the links on the page.

1 On the View menu, click Internet Options.

The Internet Options dialog box appears.

2 On the General tab, click the Colors button.

The Colors dialog box appears. The current colors being used for links are shown in the Visited and Unvisited boxes.

3 In the Links area, click the Visited color box.

The Color dialog box appears with the current color selected.

4 In the Basic Colors area, click yellow.

Your screen should look similar to the following illustration.

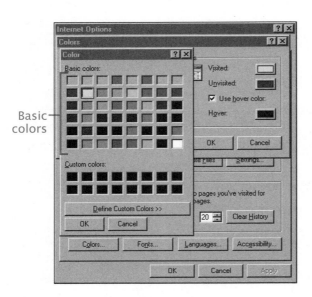

Basic colors

5 Click OK.

You might need to experiment with different colors to find a combination you like. If you want to go back to the original settings, use purple for the Visited link, use blue for the Unvisited link, and clear the Use Hover Color check box.

The Colors dialog box closes, and the new color is shown in the Visited color box.

6 In the Links area, click the Unvisited color box.

7 In the Basic Colors area, click red, and click OK.

The Colors dialog box closes, and the new color is shown in the Unvisited color box.

8 In the Links area, select the Use Hover Color check box, and then click the Hover box.

The hover color is the color the link becomes when you position the mouse pointer on it.

9 In the Basic Colors area, click blue, and click OK.

10 Click OK. Click OK again.

The new colors are applied to the links on the screen.

NOTE If you find a page where the links do not appear in the colors you selected, you can override the designer's color choices by clicking the Accessibility button in the Internet Options dialog box, and then selecting the Ignore Colors Specified On Web Pages check box.

Customizing the Toolbar

For a demonstration of how to customize a toolbar, refer to p.xxii in the Using the Microsoft Internet Explorer 4 Step by Step CD-ROM section.

For a list of Internet service types you can use in the Address bar, see Lesson 1, "Browsing the World Wide Web."

The toolbar contains separate bars that you can adjust as you use Internet Explorer. You can remove the text labels to make more room on your screen, rearrange the bars to put the ones you use most often close to the text of Web pages, or hide the bars completely so that the full screen is available for viewing Web pages.

When you start Internet Explorer, the toolbar, Address bar, and Quick Links bar are displayed. The toolbar shows the buttons that give you quick access to actions like Back, Home, and Edit as well as the Search, Favorites, History, and Channels buttons. The Address bar is used to enter Web page addresses, Autosearch commands, and file names. You also use the Address bar to reach Internet service types such as Gopher, an information retrieval system developed at the University of Minnesota that gives you access to text-only information stored on Gopher sites around the world. The Quick Links bar, labeled Links on the toolbar, lists shortcuts to a variety of Microsoft Web sites.

 NOTE   The exercises in this section show different ways you can rearrange bars on your screen. Don't worry if your screen starts to look cluttered. The final exercise shows you how to restore the bars to their original appearance.

Remove the text labels

In this exercise, you remove the text labels from the buttons on the toolbar to decrease the amount of screen space used by the toolbar.

You can also right-click a blank space on the Standard toolbar, and then click Text Labels on the shortcut menu.

1   On the View menu, point to Toolbars.

The toolbars menu is displayed. Each item with a checkmark next to it is displayed.

2   Click Text Labels.

The text labels are removed. Your toolbar should look similar to the following illustration.

Standard toolbar without text labels →

Resize the Quick Links bar

In this exercise, you increase the Quick Links bar so you can see several of the links listed on the bar. The Quick Links bar is labeled "Links" on the toolbar.

1   Position the mouse pointer on the bar next to the Links label.

     The pointer changes to a two-headed arrow.

2   Drag the Links bar to the left.

     The Links are displayed, and the Address bar is reduced in size. Your screen should look similar to the following illustration.

Expanded Quick Links bar

 WEB PICK   Science is always fun with Bill Nye the Science Guy at http://nyelabs.kcts.org

View the Web page on the full screen

In this exercise, you remove all bars from the screen and view the Web page on the full screen.

You can also click the Full Screen button on the toolbar to go into, and out of, full screen mode.

1   On the View menu, click Full Screen.

     The Web page appears in the full screen window.

2   Right-click a blank space on the toolbar.

     A shortcut menu is displayed.

3   Click Auto Hide.

     The Web page appears in the full screen.

4   To return to the regular Internet Explorer window, position the mouse pointer at the top of the Full Screen view.

     The toolbar is displayed.

5   Right-click a blank area on the toolbar.

     A shortcut menu is displayed.

6   Click Menu bar.

     The Menu bar is displayed on the toolbar.

7   Choose View, and then, on the View menu, click Full Screen.

     The toolbar, Menu bar, Links bar, and Address bar are restored.

Restore the screen to its original appearance

In this exercise, you restore the bars to their default sizes and positions on the screen.

1 Right-click a blank space on the toolbar, and then click Text Labels.

The text labels are restored on the toolbar.

2 Drag the Links bar to the right until only the word "Links" is displayed.

The screen is returned to its original appearance. Your screen should look similar to the following illustration.

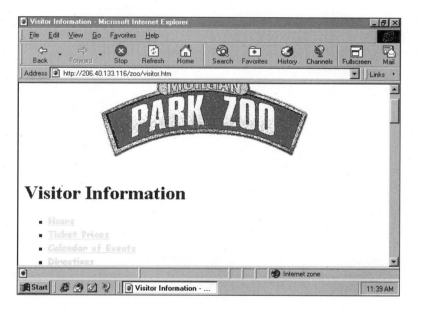

Managing Your History List

A record of the Web sites you visit is kept automatically in your History list. You can view the contents of the list and quickly access the sites from the Explorer Bar.

You can organize your History list by defining the number of days you want to save on your History list and by periodically clearing out the entries. If you find that the list has too many entries, you can delete them one at a time or all at once.

If you want to keep the site reference, add the site to your Favorites list, as described in Lesson 2.

 WEB PICK Visit great works of art online at the Louvre at http://mistral.culture.fr/louvre

Select the number of days to keep pages in History

In this exercise, you reset the number of days that you want to keep in your History list to reduce its size.

1   On the View menu, click Internet Options.

     The Internet Options dialog box appears.

2   On the General tab, in the History area, click the Days To Keep Pages In History down arrow or up arrow until you reach the desired number of days, and then click OK.

View entries on the Explorer Bar

In this exercise, you open the Explorer Bar and view a list of the sites you have visited recently using the History button.

1   On the toolbar, click History.

     The History list is displayed. Sites are grouped into different time periods.

2   On the History list, click Today.

     The list of sites you have visited is displayed. Your screen should look similar to the following illustration.

You can also click the View menu, point to Explorer Bar, and then click History.

3   On your History list, locate Morgan Park Zoo.

     A list of the pages you have visited at Morgan Park Zoo is displayed.

 IMPORTANT Morgan Park Zoo and www.highway99.com/zoo are friendly names for the Morgan Park Zoo Web site. The site might be displayed in your History list under its actual numerical URL as 206.40.133.116

4 Click the Morgan Park Zoo link, www.highway99.com/zoo or 206.40.133.116.

The main page of the Morgan Park Zoo site appears.

Delete one History item

In this exercise, you delete one site from your History list.

1 On the Explorer Bar, right-click Visitor Information.

2 On the shortcut menu, click Delete.

A Warning dialog box appears.

3 In the Warning dialog box, click Yes.

The item is deleted.

Close the Explorer Bar

You can also click the Close button on the Explorer Bar, or click the View menu, point to Explorer Bar, and then click History.

In this exercise, you close the Explorer Bar.

➤ On the toolbar, click History.

The Explorer Bar closes, and the Web page is displayed across the full width of the screen.

Clear the History list

In this exercise, you clear all sites from your History list. This is a good way to delete old files from your hard drive and keep your history list manageable.

1 On the View menu, click Internet Options.

The Internet Options dialog box appears.

2 In the History area, click Clear History.

The Internet Properties dialog box appears. If you have changed your mind and want to keep the items in your History folder, you can click No.

 NOTE When you delete items from your History folder, the items are deleted permanently. They are not moved to the Recycle Bin.

3 Click Yes.

The site and page links are deleted from the History folder.

4 Click OK.

Reviewing Your Security Zones

In Internet Explorer, you can assign Web sites to groups called security zones. With security zones, you can set up different security rules for different groups of Web sites. For example, if you purchase office supplies regularly over the Internet, you can include the office supply company's Web site in your Trusted Sites zone.

There are four security zones in Internet Explorer. The following table describes the security zones.

This security zone	Is used for
Local intranet	Sites that are part of your company's intranet. This zone is set up and maintained by your Internet Administrator.
Trusted sites	Web sites that you trust. The default security level for this zone is Low. Use this zone when you want to allow files to be downloaded or programs to be run from a site. You can assign specific Web sites to this zone.
Restricted sites	Web sites that you do not trust. This zone should be reserved for sites you know require a High security level. For example, if files you downloaded from a site contained a virus, you would assign that site to this zone.
Internet	Sites that do not fit into any other category and sites you have not previously visited and assigned to a security zone. The default security level for this zone is Medium. You cannot add sites to this zone.

 NOTE Each security zone is assigned a High, Medium, Low, or Custom level of security. The High level is the most secure, and the Low level is the least secure. You can accept the settings supplied with Internet Explorer, or you can customize the levels with your own settings. Some of the choices include enabling and disabling Active X or Java, and controlling what type of information you will allow to be downloaded to your PC. If you are not familiar with the features on the Custom list, you should use the settings supplied with Internet Explorer.

Add a site to a security zone

In this exercise, you start building your own list of Web sites in your Trusted Sites zone.

IMPORTANT To complete this exercise, you need the URL of the site you want to add.

1   On the View menu, click Internet Options.

The Internet Options dialog box appears.

2   In the Internet Options dialog box, click the Security tab.

3   Click the Zone down arrow, and then click Trusted Sites Zone.

4   In the Trusted Sites area, click Add Sites.

5   In the Trusted Sites Zone area, click in the Add This Web Site To The Zone box. Type the URL for the site that you want to add to the zone.

6   Click the Add button.

The site is listed in the Web Sites box.

7   Click OK until all dialog boxes are closed.

Remove a site from a security zone

In this exercise, you remove a site from the Trusted Sites zone.

1   On the View menu, click Internet Options.

The Internet Options dialog box appears.

2   In the Internet Options dialog box, click the Security tab.

3   Click the Zone down arrow, and then click Trusted Sites Zone.

4   In the Trusted Sites area, click Add Sites.

The site you added is listed in the Web Sites box.

5   In the Web Sites box, click the site you added in the previous exercise, and then click Remove.

The site is removed from the security zone.

6   Click OK until all dialog boxes are closed.

 NOTE If you'd like to build on the skills you learned in this lesson, you can work through the exercises in One Step Further. Otherwise, skip to "Finish the lesson."

One Step Further: Specifying Your Privacy Options

There are options in Internet Explorer that help ensure your privacy on the Internet. For example, you can indicate that you want to be notified when you switch from a secure Web site to an unsecure site. Secure sites are used on the Web primarily for financial transactions. When you access a secure site, information (such as your credit card number) is transmitted using security protocols. Receiving a warning when you switch from secure to unsecure sites helps you protect your private information.

 WEB PICK   For more information about privacy and the Internet, see the Center for Democracy and Privacy at http://www.cdt.org and the Electronic Privacy Information Center at http://www.epic.org

You can also indicate that you want to be notified when a site is going to send you a "Cookie." *Cookies* are files that are automatically sent to your computer when you visit some sites. They can be used by the site to customize your viewing of the Web site. For example, you might go to a Web site and fill in some personal information such as your name and hobbies. The next time you visit that Web site the information you stored in the Cookie can be used by the site to greet you by name or to keep track of items in your online shopping basket, making the visit more personal. Cookies do not harm files, but many people like to be notified when a site wants to send Cookies.

 TIP   You can look at the contents of Cookies files after they are sent from a site. To locate the files on your computer, search your hard drive for a file named Cookies.

Choose your privacy settings

In this exercise, you review your privacy settings to be sure that you will be warned when you switch between secure and unsecure mode on Web sites and change a setting so that you will be warned when a site wants to send Cookies.

1   On the View menu, click Internet Options.

 The Internet Options dialog box appears.

2   Click the Advanced tab.

3   Scroll down to the Security area, and be sure that the Warn If Changing Between Secure And Unsecure Mode check box is selected.

 If it is not selected, click the check box to select it.

4   Scroll down to the Cookies area.

5 In the Cookies area, select the Prompt Before Accepting Cookies check box.

When this option is enabled, a dialog box will appear when a site wants to send Cookies.

6 Click OK.

Privacy vs. Convenience

At first glance, you might be tempted to turn on all security options and restrict as many actions as possible. However, this could mean that you spend most of your time responding to warnings in dialog boxes instead of looking at interesting Web sites. You need to compare risks versus benefits and decide which security measures you are comfortable with on the Internet.

Finish the lesson

Follow these steps to reset your privacy options to the original settings and finish the lesson.

If you want to be notified when a site tries to send Cookies, skip steps 1 through 4.

1 On the View menu, click Internet Options.

2 In the Internet Options dialog box, click the Advanced tab.

3 Scroll down to the Cookies area, and select the Always Accept Cookies check box.

4 Click OK.

5 To continue to the next lesson, on the toolbar, click Home.

If you are using a network connection, skip steps 7 and 8.

6 If you are finished using Internet Explorer for now, on the File menu, click Close.

7 In the Disconnect dialog box, click Yes.

8 In the Reconnect dialog box, click No.

Lesson Summary

To	Do this
Reset the font size	On the View menu, point to Font and reset the font size.
Select link colors	On the View menu, click Internet Options. Click Colors. Click the Visited color box, select a new color, and click OK.

To	Do this	Button
Remove or restore text labels on the toolbar	On the View menu, point to Toolbars, and then click Text Labels.	
Resize a bar	Drag the bar to the left or right.	
Move a bar	Drag the label to the new location.	
View a Web page on the full screen	On the View menu, click Full Screen. Right-click the toolbar, and then click Auto Hide.	
Select the number of days to keep pages in history	On the View menu, click Internet Options. Click the Days To Keep Pages In History down arrow, and click OK.	
View or hide the History Bar	On the toolbar, click History.	History
Delete one history site	On the Explorer Bar, right-click the site. On the shortcut menu, click Delete, and then click Yes.	
Clear the History folder	On the View menu, click Internet Options. Click Clear History, click Yes, and click OK.	
Add a site to a security zone	On the View menu, click Internet Options. Click the Security tab. Click the Zone down arrow, and select a security zone. Click Add Sites. Click in the Add This Web Site To The Zone box, type the URL you want to add, and then click Add. Click OK. Click OK again.	
Remove a site from a security zone	On the View menu, click Internet Options. Click the Security tab. Click the Zone down arrow, and select a security zone. Click Add Sites. In the Web Sites box, click the site you want to remove, and then click Remove. Click OK. Click OK again.	

For online information about	On the Help menu, click Contents And Index, click the Index tab, and then type
Resetting the font size	**font size, changing**
Changing link colors	**colors**
Customizing the toolbar	**toolbar**
Viewing pages from the History folder	**history**
Adding sites to security zones	**security zones**

Review & Practice

You will review and practice how to:

- Browse a World Wide Web site.
- Search for information on the Web.
- Add a Web page to your list of Favorites.
- Display a Web page in Full Screen view.
- Manage your History folder.

Estimated time
20 min.

Before you move on to Part 2, which covers using the Active Desktop, subscribing to Web sites, and editing Web pages, you can practice the skills you learned in Part 1 by working through this Review & Practice section. You will browse through the pages on a Web site, search for new sites, and add a site that you find using Favorites. You will also view the new site on the full screen, access pages from your History list, and clear your History list.

Scenario

As a new summer intern at the Morgan Park Zoo, you have been assigned the task of compiling a list of all animal exhibits at zoos in your area. You decide to use the Web to do your research and to visit as many zoos as you can online.

Step 1:   Browse a Web Site

You have heard that your own zoo has a Web site, so you decide to start your research by visiting the site.

1   Start Internet Explorer.

2   Open the Morgan Park Zoo home page at www.highway99.com/zoo

3   Using buttons at the bottom of the home page, go to the Exhibits page.

4   Visit the Pachyderms exhibit page.

5   Go back to the Morgan Park Zoo home page.

For more information about	See
Starting Internet Explorer	Lesson 1
Opening a page by using its URL	Lesson 1
Moving from page to page	Lesson 1

Step 2:   Search for Information on the Web

You need to expand your research and locate other zoos in your area. You search the Web for other zoo sites and refine your search to focus on a specific zoo.

1   On the Internet Explorer screen, open the Search list on the Explorer Bar.

2   Select a search engine, and search for "zoos."

3   Refine your search to look for "Woodland Park Zoo."

4   Browse the Woodland Park Zoo site. (Hint: Your search might find many sites about the Woodland Park Zoo. Look for a site with the URL www.zoo.org)

For more information about	See
Opening the Search Bar	Lesson 2
Selecting a search engine	Lesson 2
Refining your search	Lesson 2
Browsing a Web site	Lesson 1

Step 3:   Add a Web Page to Your List of Favorites

As you browse the Woodland Park Zoo site, you add the page you are viewing to your list of Favorites. You create a new folder to hold your favorite Woodland Park Zoo pages.

1   Add the Woodland Park Zoo page to your list of Favorites.

2   Create a new folder called WPZ to hold the Woodland Park Zoo page.

3   Move the page you just added to your Favorites list into the new folder.

For more information about	See
Adding the current page to your list of Favorites	Lesson 2
Creating a new folder	Lesson 2
Moving your Favorites into a new folder	Lesson 2

Step 4:   *View a Web Page on the Full Screen*

As you browse the Woodland Park Zoo site, you locate animal pictures you would like to see on the full screen.

1   Display the current page in Full Screen view.

2   Hide the toolbar.

3   Restore the regular Internet Explorer screen.

For more information about	See
Viewing a Web page in Full Screen view	Lesson 3
Hiding the toolbar in Full Screen view	Lesson 3
Exiting Full Screen view and restoring the Internet Explorer screen	Lesson 3

Step 5:   *Manage Your History List*

You review your History list and notice that it is getting long as you move from page to page on zoo sites. Since the site references you want to save are stored on your Favorites list, you decide to clear the History list.

1   Open the History list.

2   View the History pages to make sure you want to delete them.

3   Clear your History list.

For more information about	See
Opening the History Bar	Lesson 3
Viewing pages from the History Bar	Lesson 3
Clearing the History list	Lesson 3

Finish the Review & Practice

Follow these steps to delete the folder you created in this Review & Practice, and then quit Internet Explorer.

1   In the Organize Favorites dialog box, delete the WPZ folder.

2   If you want to continue to the next lesson, on the toolbar, click Home.

3   If you are finished using Internet Explorer for now, on the File menu, click Close.

4   In the Disconnect dialog box, click Yes.

5   In the Reconnect dialog box, click No.

Bringing the
Web to Your PC

Activating the Web on Your PC

Estimated time
40 min.

In this lesson you will learn how to:

■ Add content from the World Wide Web to your desktop.

■ Preview channels from the Channel Bar.

■ Subscribe to Web sites.

■ View Web pages offline.

Do you like to read the newspaper first thing in the morning? Internet Explorer's Active Desktop and Web integration features bring the Web to your PC. This means Internet Explorer can deliver your local newspaper to your Desktop. And, if you leave your computer on overnight, Active Desktop automatically updates your newspaper so you can count on getting the latest news when you sit down to your computer with your morning coffee. This function, called *subscribing* to a Web page, is just one of a variety of features in Active Desktop and Web integration that make it easy for you to access the Internet from your Desktop.

One of the first things you probably noticed when you loaded Internet Explorer on your PC was the *Channel Bar*, the vertical bar on your Windows Desktop. The channels located on the Channel Bar are shortcuts to selected Web pages, and they work something like television channels. For example, like television channels, channel programming changes regularly. In addition, you choose the channels you want to view. You can view the Web pages on a channel while you are connected to the Internet, or you can set up a subscription to have the content delivered and stored on your PC so you can read it *offline*. Offline reading enables you to read Web pages from your PC without being connected to the Internet.

Internet Explorer's Web integration gives you access to the Web from anywhere on your PC. If you're working in My Computer, you can click in the *Address bar*, type in a Web site, and push ENTER. Internet Explorer will start, and the Web page will be loaded. You can also add the Address bar to the taskbar, which already contains icons for launching Internet Explorer, Outlook Express, and Channels, giving you even quicker access to the Internet regardless of where you're working on the Desktop. When the Web Integrated Desktop option is enabled, Web-related commands are also added to your Start menu and toolbars. And, it's just as easy to move from the Internet back to your Desktop using the Show Desktop icon. That way, if you're browsing the Web and someone requests a file you've saved on your Desktop, all you have to do is click the Show Desktop icon to retrieve the file. Pressing the taskbar once will return you to the Web page you were browsing.

 WEB PICK   Have you listened to the Internet lately? Try the audio interviews at the Book Radio site at http://www.bookradio.com

In your job as systems coordinator for the computer consulting firm of Ferguson and Bardell, you have to keep up-to-date on the latest computer and Web technologies. You want to use your PC as a model that shows other employees the capabilities of the Active Desktop. You also need to subscribe to Web sites so you can read professional development articles on your laptop computer during your commute to work.

Start Internet Explorer

In this exercise, you start Internet Explorer.

 IMPORTANT   To complete this lesson, you must have a dial-up connection to an Internet Service Provider or a network connection to the Internet. You must also have Internet Explorer 4 installed with Windows Desktop Update enabled. For more information on setting up your connection and installing Internet Explorer, see Appendix A, "Establishing Your Internet Connection."

You can also click the Launch Internet Explorer Browser icon on the taskbar.

1   On the Desktop, click the Internet Explorer icon.

The Internet Explorer window opens. The Microsoft Network Sign In dialog box appears, and your Member ID is displayed in the Member ID box.

If you are using a service provider other than MSN, or if you have a network connection, skip steps 2 and 3.

2 In the Password box, type your password.

If you do not want to type your password every time you connect to The Microsoft Network, select the Remember My Password check box. But remember, if you choose this option, anyone using MSN on your computer has access to your MSN account.

3 In The Microsoft Network Sign In dialog box, click Connect.

The Microsoft Network Sign In dialog box closes, and the Internet Start page appears.

4 If necessary, maximize the Internet Explorer window.

Adding the Web to Your Desktop

In Internet Explorer, the Desktop is more than just a place to store shortcuts to programs. The Desktop comes alive with information from the Web. Any animation, sound, or graphics you can view on a Web page can also be viewed from the Desktop. You can use your Desktop background to display one large Web page or to display many Web pages. You can also add items, such as a stock ticker or a 3-D rotating clock, from the Microsoft Active Desktop Gallery to your Desktop.

You can make your Desktop as active or as inactive as you want. If you like the convenience of seeing a Web page, such as your favorite newspaper or magazine, without going into Internet Explorer, add the page to your Desktop. If you go overboard and end up with a kaleidoscopic Desktop, you can always delete an item or two and experiment until you get the Desktop that is right for you.

Add a new item to the Active Desktop

The Active Desktop Gallery contains items you can add to your Desktop to bring the Desktop to life. The gallery is updated constantly, which means you can redesign your Desktop as often as you like. In this exercise, you add the MSN Investor Ticker from the Active Desktop Gallery to your Desktop. The MSN Investor Ticker is a stock ticker that scrolls across your Desktop.

Show Desktop

1 On the taskbar, click the Show Desktop button.

You can use this button to return to the Desktop at any time, without minimizing the current window.

2 On the Desktop, right-click any blank space.

A shortcut menu is displayed.

3 On the shortcut menu, point to Active Desktop, and be sure that View As Web Page is selected.

4 On the shortcut menu, click Customize My Desktop.

The Display Properties dialog box appears, and the Web tab is selected.

5 In the Items On The Active Desktop area, click New.

6 In the New Active Desktop Item dialog box, click Yes. If necessary, maximize your screen.

The Active Desktop Gallery page at the Microsoft Web site appears.

7 On the Active Desktop Gallery page, click MSN Investor Ticker.

8 Scroll down, and click the Add To My Desktop button.

The Security Alert dialog box appears.

9 In the Security Alert dialog box, click Yes.

The Add Item To Active Desktop dialog box appears.

10 In the Add Items To Active Desktop dialog box, click OK.

The installation begins. You can monitor the progress of the installation in the Downloading Subscriptions dialog box.

11 When the installation is finished, on the taskbar, click Show Desktop.

Your screen should look similar to the following illustration.

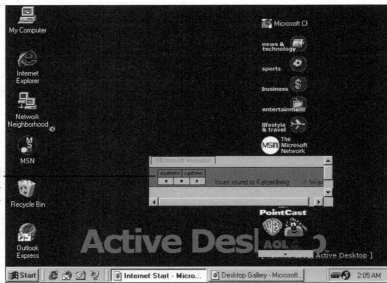

 NOTE To move the ticker on the Desktop, position the mouse pointer on the top edge of the ticker, and drag the gray border.

Display a Web page on the Active Desktop

To display a Web page on your Desktop, you first indicate that you want to customize your Desktop, then choose a page. Behind the scenes, the subscription for the page is added. You'll learn more about subscriptions later in this lesson. In this exercise, you add the Microsoft Daily News page to your Desktop.

1   On the Desktop, right-click any blank space.

  A shortcut menu is displayed.

2   On the shortcut menu, point to Active Desktop, and then click Customize My Desktop.

  The Display Properties dialog box appears, and the Web tab is selected.

3   In the Items On The Active Desktop area, click New.

4   In the New Active Desktop Item dialog box, click No.

5   In the Location area, type **http://www.microsoft.com/windows/ dailynews2/** and click OK.

  The Add Item To Active Desktop dialog box appears. The Web page is updated automatically according to either a schedule set by the publisher of the page or to the default daily update setting of 12 AM.

6   In the Add Item To Active Desktop dialog box, click OK.

  By default, the page is *downloaded*, which means the page is copied from the Web to your PC. The Downloading Subscriptions dialog box appears as the page is downloaded.

7   In the Display Properties dialog box, click OK.

  The Microsoft Daily News Web page appears in a small frame on the Desktop. You can use the scroll bars on the frame to view more text, or you can enlarge the frame to see more text.

8   Position the mouse pointer on any edge of the page, and drag the border to resize the page.

9   Position the mouse pointer on the top gray border of the MS Daily News page, and drag the page up so that all desktop elements are visible.

  The page is positioned in the upper-left corner of the screen.

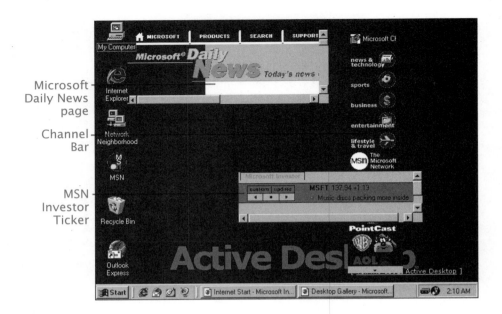

Microsoft Daily News page

Channel Bar

MSN Investor Ticker

Add the Address bar to the taskbar

In addition to customizing your Desktop with gallery items and Web pages, you can also customize your taskbar. You're already familiar with how to use the Address bar in Internet Explorer; why not use this knowledge on your Desktop by adding the Address bar to your taskbar? You can use the Address bar to enter Web page URLs, open files on your PC or your company's network, or access other Internet services such as telnet or ftp. In this exercise, you add the Address bar to your taskbar.

1   Right-click a blank area on the taskbar.

A shortcut menu is displayed.

2   On the shortcut menu, point to Toolbars, and then click Address.

The Address bar is added to the taskbar.

Subscribing to Web Pages

Staying up-to-date with the information available on the Web can be time-consuming. To make it easier to keep up with new information, you can subscribe to Web pages. Subscribing means you can be notified when information on a page is updated. You can also have the updated information delivered automatically to your PC and read it offline without connecting to the Internet.

NOTE This process is called a "subscription" only because you are having content delivered; there is no fee involved.

When you subscribe to a Web page, you let Internet Explorer search pages for you and notify you when a page has been updated. You can subscribe to one page or to a page and the pages linked to it. How do you know when a page has been updated? If the page is on your Favorites list, a red "gleam" appears on the page's link. If you indicate on the subscription you want to be notified by e-mail, a message is sent to your e-mail Inbox. If you select the download option on the subscription, the new information is downloaded and stored on your PC. If you miss the notification, you can always look up the subscription in your Subscriptions folder and see when it was last updated.

You can have two subscriptions to any Web page on your Favorites list, or you can subscribe to *channels*. A channel is a special Web page set up to deliver content to subscribers.

Subscribing to a Favorites Page or a Channel: What's the Difference?

Deciding whether to subscribe to a page on your Favorites list or to subscribe to a channel can be confusing. The two types of subscriptions are very similar. Both types use the same Daily, Weekly, Monthly, and Custom schedules; both types allow you to access new information from the Desktop or the Internet Explorer screen; and both types download information to your PC so you can read it offline.

Where the two types differ is how new information is gathered. With a Favorites subscription, a *Site Crawl* program goes through the pages you have subscribed to, looking for new information. On a channel subscription, the author of the Web site determines which pages will be delivered to your PC and sets up a schedule for delivery. With channels, the author can manage the amount of content that is delivered to keep subscribers from being overwhelmed with information.

Some people like the managed flow of information achieved through channel subscriptions; others prefer to subscribe to a Favorites page and sort through the data themselves. The choice is up to you. The subscription process is flexible; you can add a Favorites subscription to one Web page and a channel subscription to another.

Scheduling Updates

There are three scheduling options available when you subscribe to a Web page. The following table describes when you should use each option.

Scheduling option	Use this option when
Publisher's recommended schedule	You want the subscription to be updated automatically according to a schedule determined by the page's publisher or according to a default update setting.
Custom schedule	You want the subscription updated according to a Weekly, Monthly, or another schedule.
Manually	You do not want the subscription updated on a schedule. With this option, you will have to update the subscription on your own.

The pages you subscribe to are scanned according to the schedule you assign. You can choose a Daily, Weekly, Monthly, or Custom schedule and indicate a specific time of day the pages should be accessed. For example, you can set up your Daily schedule to run at noon every other day, your Weekly schedule to run at 8:00 AM on Mondays, or your Monthly schedule to run at midnight on the first day of the month.

You can set the frequency and time of day that works best for you. When you set up your schedules, keep in mind that your computer must be able to connect to the Internet at the scheduled times so that the Web pages can be accessed.

Receiving Information Through Channels

The most convenient way to subscribe to a channel is to preview the channels that come with Internet Explorer on the Channel Guide. Most channels offer selections and allow you to customize the type of information you receive.

Any Web site can be a channel. Sites contain a *Channel Definition Format* (CDF) file, which provides a list of the Web pages scheduled for delivery and can include optional information such as a delivery schedule, the hierarchy of the Web site, or abstracts describing the Web pages. You won't see a CDF file, or even know that it is there, when you read a Web page. The file is used only to help the site's owner indicate what information should be delivered to subscribers on the channel.

Subscribe to a channel

In this exercise, you open the Channel Guide, look for channels that deliver news about computers, and subscribe to the CMPnet channel.

1 On the Desktop, locate the Channel Bar.

2 On the Channel Bar, click Channel Guide and then click Yes.

If the Microsoft Internet Explorer Welcome dialog box appears, click No to proceed with the lesson. The channel preview page appears on the Channel Viewer screen, and the Channel Guide is displayed.

To stop the Explorer Bar from sliding off the left side of the screen, click the Push Pin icon at the top of the Explorer Bar. You have to be fast because it moves quickly.

3 On the Channel Guide, click the News & Technology category.

 TIP On the left side of the screen, you can position the mouse pointer on each provider's name to see a brief statement about the provider's content in a ToolTip box.

---

4 On the left side of the screen, scroll down, and click CMPnet.

The CMPnet page appears.

CMPnet page

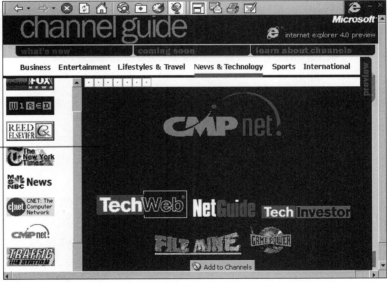

Some channels offer screen savers. If you get a screen saver dialog box when you subscribe to a channel, make the desired selections.

5 On the CMPnet page, scroll down, and click Add To Channels.

The Add Active Channel Content dialog box appears.

6 Be sure that the Yes, Notify Me Of Updates And Download The Channel For Offline Viewing option is selected, and click OK.

The Please Wait: Page Loading message appears. Your subscription to the CMPnet page is added. The CMPnet page appears.

7 When you are finished reading the CMPnet page, on the Explorer Bar window, close the Channel Viewer window.

The CMPnet entry is added to the Channel Bar on your Desktop. If the CMPnet entry is not visible, you might need to click the down arrow on the lower border of the Channel Bar to see more channels.

Adding a Subscription to a Favorites Page

You can subscribe to a new page that you want to add to your Favorites list or to a page already on your Favorites list. Your subscription applies to one Web page. If you want to expand the subscription to include pages linked to the main page, you can subscribe to multiple levels of pages. The main page is level 1. The more levels you download, the more information you will receive.

You'll learn how to manage the downloaded information in the "Revising a Subscription" section later in this lesson.

Sometimes, you can get too much of a good thing. If you find you are receiving too much new information, you can reduce the number of levels, limit the download to only the main Web page, omit image or audio files, or set a maximum download file size.

Subscribe to a new Favorites page

In this exercise, you add the Internet Explorer Web page to your list of Favorites and subscribe to the page.

1 On the taskbar, click in the Address box.

2 Type **www.microsoft.com/ie** and press ENTER.

The Internet Explorer page appears in a new Internet Explorer window.

3 If necessary, maximize the new Internet Explorer window.

4 On the Favorites menu, click Add To Favorites.

The Add To Favorites dialog box appears.

5 Select the Yes, Notify Me Of Updates And Download The Page For Offline Viewing option, and click OK.

Subscribe to a site already on your Favorites list

In this exercise, you subscribe to a site on your Favorites list.

1 On the toolbar, click Favorites.

The Explorer Bar and your list of Favorites are displayed.

2 On the Explorer Bar, click the page to which you want to subscribe.

TIP If you have not added any of your own Favorites, you can use one of the links supplied with Internet Explorer. On the Favorites list, click the Links folder, and then click Product News.

You can also right-click the link on the Favorites list, and then click Subscribe.

3 On the Favorites menu, click Organize Favorites.

The Organize Favorites dialog box appears.

4 Right-click a site you want to subscribe to, and click Subscribe.

The Subscribe Favorite dialog box appears.

5 Select the Notify Me Of Updates And Download The Page For Offline Viewing option, click OK, and then click Close.

The subscription is added.

6 On the toolbar, click Favorites.

The Explorer Bar closes.

Updating Subscriptions Manually

If you do not log on to the Internet daily, or if you log on at different times every day, you can manually update your subscriptions to be sure you don't miss any new information by skipping a scheduled update.

You'll learn how to read e-mail messages in Outlook Express in Lesson 6.

All of the subscriptions you've added so far have been primed to update automatically. If you do not want to wait for the regular update, you can update a subscription manually by designating when you want information delivered to your Desktop.

You can perform a manual update as often as you want. This is a quick way to check a site for new information. The update process runs in the background, so you can continue to do other work on your PC while the process is running. You can update subscriptions manually one at a time or all at once.

If you've subscribed to a site on your Favorites list and the manual update locates new information, a red "gleam" will appear next to the page on the Favorites list. You can click the link on the Favorites list to read the page. When you added the subscription, if you indicated that you wanted to be notified by e-mail, a message will be waiting in your Inbox the next time you go into Outlook Express. You can click on the page's link in your e-mail message to read the page.

Update one subscription manually

In this exercise, you manually update the subscription to the Internet Explorer Home page.

You can also right-click a subscription on the Favorites list, and then click Update Now, or right-click a channel on the Channel Bar, and then click Update Now.

1 On the Favorites menu, click Manage Subscriptions.

 NOTE Even though you access the Subscription window from the Favorites menu, you can update all subscriptions (Favorites and Channels) in the Subscriptions window.

2 In the Subscriptions window, right-click the subscription you want to update.

A shortcut menu is displayed.

3 On the shortcut menu, click Update Now.

The Downloading Subscriptions dialog box appears. Your screen should look similar to the following illustration.

Download progress —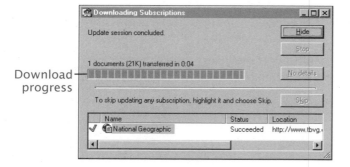

4 When the download process is complete, close the Subscriptions window.

> **NOTE** Since you just added the subscription to the Internet Explorer Home page in a previous exercise, there probably won't be any new information located by this update.

Update all subscriptions manually

If you'd prefer not to see the Downloading Subscriptions dialog box as the subscriptions are updated, you can click the Hide button on the Downloading Subscriptions dialog box.

In this exercise, you decide you do not want to wait for the scheduled updates, so you manually update all subscriptions.

1 On the Favorites menu, click Update All Subscriptions.

The Downloading Subscriptions dialog box appears.

2 In the Downloading Subscriptions dialog box, click Details.

You can monitor the progress as each site is updated. The update process might take a while, depending on the number of subscriptions you have. When the process is complete, the Downloading Subscriptions dialog box closes automatically, and your subscriptions are updated.

Viewing Subscription Pages

After you have entered your subscriptions and updated them, you'll want to view the pages. You can always view pages while you are *online,* or connected to the Internet. But, if you want to view pages offline, you must be sure the subscription indicates you want the page downloaded to your PC.

How you access pages you've subscribed to is the same whether you are reading the page online or offline. If you are offline and accidentally click a link for a page not stored on your PC, you receive notification and Internet Explorer attempts to connect you to the Internet.

Internet Explorer and the Active Desktop are set up so you can conveniently view subscription pages from a variety of locations. For example, you can view Favorites pages from the Favorites menu on the taskbar or from the Explorer Bar in Internet Explorer. The following table describes the different ways you can access subscription pages.

To	Do this
View a Favorites subscription page from the Desktop	On the taskbar, click the Start button. Point to Favorites, and then click the page you want to read. If there is new information on the page, a "gleam" appears on the link on the Favorites list.
View a Favorites subscription page from Internet Explorer	In Internet Explorer, on the toolbar, click Favorites. On your list of Favorites, click the page you want to read. Pages with new information are marked with a "gleam."
View a Channel subscription from the Channel Bar on the Desktop	On the Desktop, on the Channel Bar, click the channel you want to read.
View a Channel subscription page in Channel Viewer	On the taskbar, click the View Channels button. On the Channel Bar, click the channel you want to read.
View a Channel subscription from Internet Explorer	In Internet Explorer, on the toolbar, click Channels. On the Explorer Bar, click the channel you want to read.

If you've specified you want your subscription pages downloaded to your PC, the downloaded information is stored in your Temporary Internet Files folder. Storing pages offline is a good way to reduce your Internet connection time (if your Internet Service Provider charges by the minute or by the hour) or read Web pages when you don't have access to the Internet. When you store subscription pages offline, you don't have to worry about saving the Web page and each separate file used on the page, the way you do when you save a Web page to disk. The complete page is automatically stored in your temporary files folder. This folder is used as a temporary storage area, and you can periodically clean it out to make room for new subscription pages.

 WEB PICK Planning a trip? See http://www.traveler.net for all things travel-related.

View your favorite subscription pages while offline

In this exercise, you view your updated Favorites subscriptions offline in Internet Explorer.

If you are using a network connection, skip steps 1 and 2.

1 On the taskbar, right-click The Microsoft Network icon.

A shortcut menu is displayed.

2 On the shortcut menu, click Sign Out, and then click Yes to disconnect from The Microsoft Network.

 NOTE You can stay disconnected from the Internet for the remainder of this lesson.

Work Offline

3 On the Internet Explorer screen, on the File menu, click Work Offline.

The Work Offline icon is displayed on the status bar.

4 On the toolbar, click Favorites.

Your list of Favorites is displayed on the Explorer Bar.

5 On the Explorer Bar, click the Internet Explorer Home page.

The page is displayed in its entirety, even though you are not connected to the Internet. On your list of Favorites, the Internet Explorer Home page has a gleam if there is new information to view.

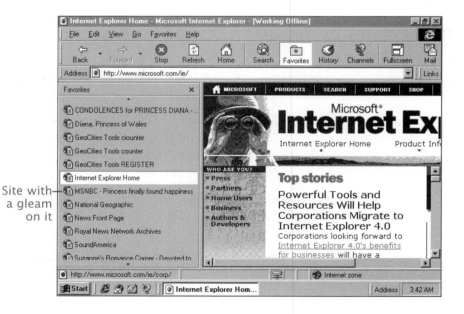

Site with a gleam on it

> **TIP** You can read more than just subscription pages offline. Information from the pages you have visited recently is also stored in the Temporary Internet Files. To read these pages, on the toolbar, click History, and then click the page you want to read.

6 On the toolbar, click Favorites.

The Explorer Bar closes.

View channel subscriptions offline

In this exercise, you view channel subscriptions offline in the Channel Viewer.

View Channels

1 On the taskbar, click the View Channels button.

2 On the Explorer Bar, click the CMPnet channel.

The CMPnet page appears. You can use the scroll bars to view more of the text.

3 When you are finished reading, close the Channel Viewer window.

Revising a Subscription

If you don't like the selections you made when you added a subscription, they can always be modified or canceled. In the subscriptions you added during this lesson, you used the default settings. In this section, you learn how to modify those settings and customize your subscriptions.

There are a lot of options available for managing how often subscriptions are updated and what types of information are downloaded to your PC. For example, if you don't like an update schedule, you can change the frequency and time of day updates are performed. Is too much information being downloaded to your PC? You can omit sound or graphics files from your downloaded pages or set a maximum file size for downloads. Are you receiving too little information? You can choose to have more linked pages downloaded. You can customize your subscriptions and schedules until you find the mix that works best for you.

Customize your Daily schedule

In this exercise, you customize the Daily schedule to change the number of days between updates and the time of day updates are performed.

1 On the Favorites menu, click Manage Subscriptions.

2   In the Subscriptions window, right-click the Internet Explorer Home subscription.

A shortcut menu is displayed.

3   On the shortcut menu, click Properties.

The Internet Explorer Home Properties dialog box appears.

4   In the Internet Explorer Home Properties dialog box, click the Schedule tab.

5   In the How Should The Subscription Be Updated area, click Edit.

6   In the Custom Schedule dialog box, in the Days area, click the Every up arrow until 3 is displayed.

This setting indicates how often the subscription will be updated. A "3" in the Every box indicates the subscription will be updated every three days.

7   In the Time area, in the Update At box, type 10:00 AM, or click the Update At up arrow until 10:00 AM is displayed.

This setting establishes the time of day of the update.

If you are using a network connection, skip step 8.

8   Clear the Varies Exact Time Of Next Update To Improve Performance check box.

When you clear this check box, your updates will be performed at the exact time listed in the Update At box. You want to set an exact time to be sure you are connected to the Internet at the scheduled update time. Your screen should look similar to the following illustration.

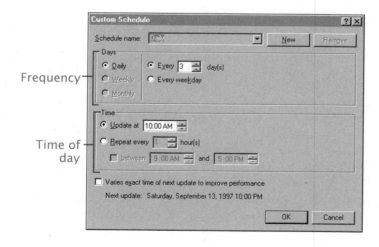

TIP   If you are adding a site subscription to a page that is on your company's intranet, you might want to select the Repeat Every option and have the page updated every one or two hours.

9   In the Custom Schedule dialog box, click OK.

10   In the How Should The Subscription Be Updated area, select the Dial As Needed If Connected Through A Modem check box, click OK, and click OK again.

Your Daily schedule is reset to update subscriptions every three days at 10:00 AM, and the Internet Explorer Home page is changed to the Daily schedule.

The change to the Daily schedule applies to all subscriptions assigned a Daily schedule.

Change a subscription from a Daily schedule to a Weekly schedule

In this exercise, you change the Internet Explorer Home subscription from a Daily schedule to a Weekly schedule.

1   In the Subscriptions window, right-click the Internet Explorer Home subscription, and then click Properties.

The status of the subscription is displayed. Your screen should look similar to the following illustration.

Status of Subscription

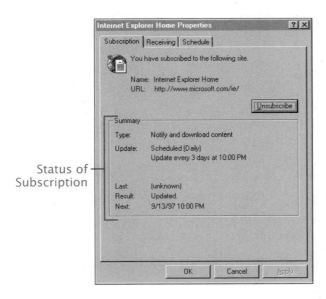

2   In the Properties dialog box, click the Schedule tab.

3 In the How Should The Subscription Be Updated area, click the Scheduled down arrow and click Weekly.

The Weekly Schedule is displayed.

4 Be sure that the Dial As Needed If Connected Through A Modem check box is selected.

5 In the Internet Explorer Home Properties dialog box, click OK.

Change the download options for a subscription

In this exercise, you reduce the amount of information downloaded from the CMPnet page by indicating that you do not want images downloaded to your PC.

1 In the Subscriptions window, right-click the CMPnet subscription, and then click Properties.

2 In the CMPnet Properties dialog box, click the Receiving tab.

3 In the Subscription Type area, click Advanced.

4 In the Items To Download area, clear the Images check box.

5 In the Advanced Download Options dialog box, click OK.

6 In the CMPnet Properties dialog box, click OK.

WEB PICK   See if your local newspaper is online by checking the newspapers list at Yahoo! at http://www.yahoo.com/News/Newspapers

Delete a subscription

In this exercise, you delete the subscriptions you added during this lesson.

You can also position the mouse pointer on the subscription you want to delete, and then click the Delete button on the toolbar. The Unsubscribe button in the Properties dialog box also deletes a subscription.

1 In the Subscriptions window, right-click the Internet Explorer Home subscription.

2 On the shortcut menu, click Delete.

3 In the Confirm Item Delete dialog box, click Yes.

4 In the Subscriptions window, right-click the CMPnet subscription.

5 On the shortcut menu, click Delete.

6 In the Confirm Item Delete dialog box, click Yes.

7 Close the Subscriptions window.

The subscriptions are deleted. The link to the Internet Explorer Home page remains on your Favorites list, and the CMPnet entry stays on the Channel Bar.

TIP If you leave the entries on your Favorites list and the Channel Bar, you'll be able to quickly go to the pages, even though you aren't subscribing to the pages.

NOTE If you'd like to build on the skills that you learned in this lesson, you can work through the exercises in One Step Further. Otherwise, skip to "Finish the lesson."

One Step Further: Deleting the Temporary Internet Files

Your Temporary Internet Files folder holds the updated subscription pages downloaded to your PC and the pages in your History folder. The Temporary Internet Files folder includes the text, graphic, sound, video, and any other files included as part of a Web page. This folder can grow quickly, and you should delete the contents periodically to make room for new pages.

After you delete the Temporary Internet Files, you will not be able to view pages offline until your subscriptions are updated or until you rebuild your History file by accessing Web pages in Internet Explorer.

Deleting the Temporary Internet Files does not delete a subscription or a link on your Favorites list.

Delete the temporary Internet files

In this exercise, you delete the files in the Temporary Internet Files folder to gain disk space for the next time your subscriptions are updated.

1   On the View menu, click Internet Options.

2   In the Temporary Internet Files area, click Delete Files.

The Delete Files dialog box appears.

3   Select the Delete All Subscription Content check box, and click OK.

The files are deleted.

4   In the Internet Options dialog box, click OK.

The dialog box closes.

Finish the lesson

In this exercise, you delete the Internet Explorer Home page from your Favorites list, delete the CMPnet entry from the Channel Bar, and restore the Desktop to its original appearance.

1   In Internet Explorer, on the toolbar, click Favorites.

2   On the Explorer Bar, right-click the Internet Explorer Home link on the list of Favorites.

3   On the shortcut menu, click Delete.

4   In the Confirm File Delete dialog box, click Yes.

The Internet Explorer Home page is deleted from your Favorites folder.

5   On the File menu, click Close.

6   On the taskbar, click the open Internet Explorer window.

7   In Internet Explorer, on the File menu, click Close.

8   On the Desktop, right-click any blank space, point to Active Desktop, and then click Customize My Desktop.

9   In the Display Properties dialog box, verify that the Web tab is selected.

10   In the Items On The Active Desktop area, click the MSN Investor Ticker, and then click Delete.

11   In the Active Desktop Item dialog box, click Yes.

12   In the Items On The Active Desktop area, click http://www.microsoft.com/windows/dailynews2/ and then click Delete.

13   In the Active Desktop Item dialog box, click Yes.

14   In the Display Properties dialog box, click OK.

The items are removed from your Desktop.

15   On the Channel Bar, right-click CMPnet, and then click Delete.

16   In the Confirm Folder Delete dialog box, click Yes.

17   Right-click the taskbar, point to Toolbars, and then click Address.

The Address bar is removed from the taskbar.

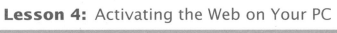

Lesson Summary

To	Do this
Add a new item to the Active Desktop	On the Desktop, right-click any blank space, point to Active Desktop, and then click Customize My Desktop. Verify that the Web tab is selected. Click New. Click Yes to add an item from the Active Desktop Gallery. Select an item, and then click Add To My Desktop. In the Security Alert message box, click Yes. In the Add Items To Active Desktop Content dialog box, click OK.
Display a Web page on the Active Desktop	On the Desktop, right-click any blank space, point to Active Desktop, and then click Customize My Desktop. Verify that the Web tab is selected. Click New. Click No, type a URL of your choice in the Location area, and click OK. In the Add Items To Active Desktop dialog box, click OK. On the Desktop, drag the border to resize the frame.
Add the Address bar to the Desktop	Right-click a blank area on the taskbar, point to Toolbars, and then click Address.
Subscribe to a channel	On the Channel Bar, click Channel Guide. On the Channel Guide, click a category. On the left side of the screen, click a channel. Once the page loads, click Add To Channels. In the Subscribe dialog box, click OK. Close the Channel Viewer window.
Subscribe to a new Favorites page	On the Favorites menu, click Add To Favorites. In the Add To Favorites dialog select the Yes, Notify Me Of Updates And Download The Page For Offline Viewing option, and click OK.

To	Do this	Button
Subscribe to a site already on your Favorites list	On the toolbar, click Favorites. On the Explorer Bar, click the page to which you want to subscribe. On the Favorites menu, click Organize Favorites, right-click the site to which you want to subscribe, and click Subscribe. In the Subscribe dialog box, select the Notify Me Of Updates And Download The Page For Offline Viewing option. Click OK, and then click Close. On the toolbar, click Favorites.	
Manually update one subscription	In Internet Explorer, on the Favorites menu, click Manage Subscriptions. Right-click the site you want to update, and then click Update Now.	
Manually update all subscriptions	On the Favorites menu, click Update All Subscriptions.	
View your favorite subscription pages offline	On the taskbar, right-click your modem icon. On the shortcut menu, click Sign Out, and then click Yes to disconnect from the Internet. In Internet Explorer, on the File menu, click Work Offline. On the toolbar, click Favorites. On the Explorer Bar, click a site that you have marked for offline reading. On the toolbar, click Favorites.	
View channel subscriptions offline	On the taskbar, click View Channels. On the Channel Bar, click the channel you want to view. Close the Channel Viewer window.	

To	Do this
Customize your Daily schedule	On the Favorites menu, click Manage Subscriptions. Right-click the subscription you want to edit. On the shortcut menu, click Properties. Click the Schedule tab, and then click Edit. In the Days area, click the Every up or down arrow until you reach the interval you want. In the Time area, click the Update At up or down arrow until you reach the time of day you want. Be sure the Varies Exact Time Of Next Update To Improve Performance check box is cleared. In the Custom Schedule dialog box, click OK. In the Internet Explorer Home Properties dialog box, in the How Should The Subscription Be Updated area, select the Dial As Needed If Connected Through A Modem check box, and click OK.
Change a subscription from the Daily schedule to the Weekly schedule	In the Subscriptions window, right-click the subscription you want to change, and then click Properties. Click the Schedule tab. Click the Scheduled down arrow, and then click Weekly. In the Properties dialog box, click OK.
Change the download options on a subscription	In the Subscriptions window, right-click the subscription you want to change. On the shortcut menu, click Properties. Click the Receiving tab. In the Downloading area, click Advanced. In the Advanced Download Options dialog box, clear the Images check box, and click OK. In the Properties dialog box, click OK.
Delete a subscription	In the Subscriptions window, right-click the subscription you want to delete, and then click Delete. In the Confirm Item Delete dialog box, click Yes.

For online information about	On the Help menu, click Contents And Index, click the Index tab, and then type
Adding items to the Desktop	Desktop
Placing the Address bar on the taskbar	Address bar
Adding a channel subscription	subscribing to channels
Adding a subscription to a Favorite Web page	subscribing to Web sites
Reading Web pages offline	offline browsing
Revising subscriptions	subscriptions

Using Files from the Web

Estimated time
35 min.

In this lesson you will learn how to:

- Print a page from the World Wide Web.
- Save a Web page to disk.
- Edit a Web page in FrontPage Express.
- Create your own Web page.

Now that you are moving around comfortably on the Internet, you will find pages you want to print or save for future reference. Printing a page is a good way to keep a record of important information and to share information with others who do not have Internet access. Saving a page also allows you to view the page on screen from a computer that is not connected to the Internet.

As you become more familiar with Web pages, you might want to edit a page or even create your own personal Web page. You can edit and create pages using the FrontPage Express program included with Internet Explorer. Web pages are formatted using HTML codes. These codes determine how the text will be displayed on the web page. With FrontPage Express, you can create pages using the options on the menus and toolbars so you don't have to learn or memorize HTML codes.

WEB PICK   The World Wide Web Consortium is a great source of information on HTML codes, proposed changes to HTML, and the history and future of HTML. You can visit the consortium's site at http://www.w3.org

In your role as systems coordinator at Ferguson and Bardell, you are considering relocating to the Western Division office to work for clients who are setting up corporate *intranets*. An intranet is a closed network that uses the same protocols as the Internet, but is confined to a specific population, usually within one company. You explore the Web to find information about intranets and save the Western Division's Web page so you can view it from your disk. You also update the Western Division Web page and create your own Web page to introduce yourself.

Start Internet Explorer

IMPORTANT   To complete this lesson, you must have a dial-up connection to an Internet Service Provider or a network connection to the Internet. You must also have Internet Explorer 4 installed. For more information on setting up your connection and installing Internet Explorer, see Appendix A, "Establishing Your Internet Connection."

You can also click the Launch Internet Explorer Browser icon on the taskbar.

1   On the Desktop, click The Internet Explorer icon.

The Internet Explorer window opens. The Microsoft Network Sign In dialog box appears, and your Member ID is displayed in the Member ID box.

2   In the Password box, type your password.

If you are using a service provider other than MSN, or if you have a network connection, skip steps 2 and 3.

If you do not want to type your password every time you connect to The Microsoft Network, select the Remember My Password check box. But remember, if you choose this option, anyone using MSN on your computer has access to your MSN account.

3   In The Microsoft Network Sign In dialog box, click Connect.

The Microsoft Network Sign In dialog box closes, and the Internet Start page appears.

4   If necessary, maximize the Internet Explorer window.

Printing a Web Page

In Internet Explorer, you can print a Web page as it looks on the screen, or you can choose to print selected *frames*. Frames are a formatting option used on some Web pages to divide the page into separate sections. For example, a Web page with two frames can display the Table of Contents in one frame and the site's home page in another.

NOTE On the screen, frames look similar to the Explorer Bar, which you use to search for information or display your list of Favorites. However, the Explorer Bar is a separate browser control built into Internet Explorer and is not a frame.

You can choose how a page constructed in frames will print. For example, you can print a selected frame, print all frames individually or print all frames the way they appear on the screen.

On all pages, whether or not they contain frames, you can print only the page, the page and all pages linked to it, or the page with a list of the links contained on the page. Printing a list of links is a good way to see what kind of additional information is available from the page without using a lot of printer time and paper to print the full text of the linked pages.

In your job at Ferguson and Bardell, you have been asked to gather information about intranets. Since you are not familiar with printing frames, you decide to explore the different print options available in Internet Explorer.

IMPORTANT Your computer must be connected to a printer for you to complete all of the exercises in this section.

Print a selected frame

In this exercise, you locate information on the Web about intranets and print the frame containing the text on the Intranet Solutions Center page.

1   On the Address bar, type **www.microsoft.com/intranet** and press ENTER.

    The Intranet Solutions Center page appears.

2   On the Intranet Solutions Center page, select the first few words in the first paragraph of text.

    By selecting text, you are indicating which frame you want to print.

3   On the File menu, click Print.

    The Print dialog box appears. Your screen should look similar to the following illustration.

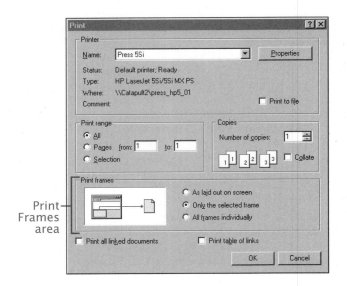

Print
Frames
area

If you don't want to print, click cancel.

4 In the Print Frames area, be sure that Only The Selected Frame option is selected, and click OK.

The frame in which the text is displayed is printed.

Print each frame on a separate page

In this exercise, you print the complete Intranet Solutions Center page with each frame printed separately.

1 On the File menu, click Print.

The Print dialog box appears.

2 In the Print Frames area, select All Frames Individually, and click OK.

Each frame is printed on a separate page.

Print a list of the linked pages

In this exercise, you print a table of links that shows the title and URL of the pages linked to the Intranet Solutions Center page.

1 On the File menu, click Print.

The Print dialog box appears.

2 In the Print dialog box, select Print Table Of Links.

NOTE If you want to see the text of the linked pages, you can select Print All Linked Documents, which prints the current page and every page linked to it.

3 In the Print dialog box, click OK.

The current page and the table of links are printed.

Print the entire page

In this exercise, you generate a printout that shows the page as it looks on the screen.

1 On the File menu, click Print.

The Print dialog box appears.

2 In the Print Frames area, select As Laid Out On Screen, and click OK.

The page is printed using the same layout you see on the screen.

Printing from the Toolbar

The fastest way to print a Web page is to use the Print button on the Standard toolbar. The page is printed immediately, and you cannot change any print settings. The page is printed as it looks on the screen, and you receive one copy of the printout on your default printer.

 NOTE If you cannot see all of the icons on your toolbar, you need to change your monitor resolution settings. Please see your owner's manual for information on this process.

Print from the toolbar

In this exercise, you print the Intranet Solutions Center page using the default printer settings.

 ➤ On the toolbar, click Print.

The page is printed.

Saving a Web Page

Web pages can contain different types of files, including sound files, graphics, or multimedia files. When you save a Web page, you must save each file used to construct the page. For example, if the page includes two graphics files, you must save the Web page itself to store the page structure and text, and then save each graphics file separately.

Copyright on the Internet

All Web page contents are copyrighted. Most Web pages include a copyright statement at the bottom of the site's home page, but even if there is no copyright statement listed, the information is still copyrighted. If you want to use something from the site, you should write to the site's contact person and obtain permission. Almost all Web pages have an e-mail link you can use to contact the site.

Occasionally, you might find a site where people have posted information or graphics to share with the public. If it is stated at the site that you can copy materials for your own use, you can save the page without obtaining permission.

 IMPORTANT To complete this exercise, you must have the practice files installed. For more information, see the "Installing and Using the Practice Files" section earlier in this book.

Save a Web page

You want to take the Western Division Web page home with you so you can reconstruct it on your home computer. In this exercise, you save the Western Division Web page to your computer.

For the sake of this exercise, you will practice saving Web pages from the practice files. Under ordinary circumstances, you would be saving from the World Wide Web.

1 On the Address bar, type **c:\Internet Explorer 4 SBS Practice\Western.htm** and press ENTER.

2 On the File menu, click Save As.

The Save HTML Document dialog box appears.

3 In the Save In box, select the Internet Explorer 4 SBS Practice folder.

4 In the File Name box, type **Ferguson and Bardell**.

5 In the Save As Type box, be sure that HTML File is displayed.

6 Click Save.

The HTML file is saved under the file name Ferguson and Bardell.htm.

Save a graphic

In this exercise, you save the picture of the eagle included on the Western Division page.

1 On the Western Division page, right-click the picture of the eagle.

A shortcut menu is displayed.

2 On the shortcut menu, click Save Picture As.

The Save Picture dialog box appears.

3 In the File Name box, type **soaring eagle**

4 In the Save Picture dialog box, be sure that Internet Explorer 4 SBS Practice is displayed, and then click Save.

NOTE The graphics file is stored on your disk under the file name soaring eagle.jpg. *JPG* stands for Joint Photographic Experts Group. JPG and *GIF*, Graphics Interchange Format, are the two most common graphic formats used on the Web.

Save the background

In this exercise, you save the graphic file used as the background on the Western Division page.

1 On the Western Division page, right-click anywhere on the light blue background.

A shortcut menu is displayed.

2 On the shortcut menu, click Save Background As.

3 In the File Name box, type **background**

4 In the Save Picture dialog box, be sure that Internet Explorer 4 SBS Practice is displayed, and click Save.

The background file is saved under the file name background.gif.

View the saved page from the Practice folder

In this exercise, you read the Western Division page from the Practice folder to be sure that you have copied all of the elements required for the page.

➤ On the Address bar, type **c:\Internet Explorer 4 SBS Practice\Ferguson and Bardell.htm** and press ENTER.

Substitute the correct drive letter if "c:" is not the letter of your disk drive. The page should look exactly the way it looked on the Web. To transport the files to a different computer, you can copy the files to a diskette.

Editing Web Pages

Editing a Web page is as easy as editing a text file on your computer. You can edit the Web page to include the text and graphics you want and use FrontPage Express to insert the HTML codes.

If you like to see the "nuts and bolts" behind the formatting, you can view the HTML codes in Internet Explorer or in FrontPage Express. The following illustrations show the Western Division Web page as it appears on the regular screen in FrontPage Express, and as it appears when you view the HTML codes.

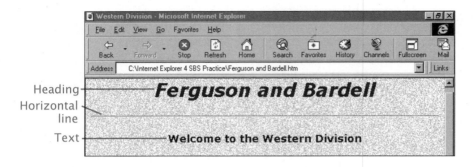

Heading

Horizontal line

Text

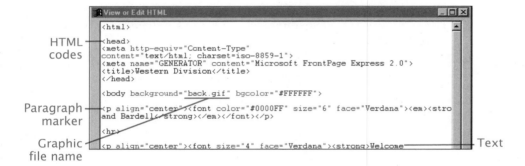

HTML codes

Paragraph marker

Graphic file name

Text

In this section, you edit the Western Division Web page and add a graphic and text to the page. When you edit a Web page, you cannot publish the edited version on the Web unless you have security access to modify the page. For example, you can type the Western Division Web page URL in Internet Explorer and edit the page in FrontPage Express, but you cannot publish your edited version on the Web. Only the people who are authorized to publish that page can post it back to the Web. You can save the edited page to your disk, which you will do in this section.

For a demonstration of how to insert a graphics file, refer to p.xxii in the Using the Microsoft Internet Explorer 4 Step by Step CD-ROM section.

Insert a graphics file

You have been asked by the Western Division staff to update their Web page with information about intranets. In this exercise, you insert an announcement about the upcoming Intranet Services Department.

1 Be sure that **c:\Internet Explorer 4 SBS Practice\Ferguson and Bardell.htm** is displayed in the Address box.

You can also click Page on the Edit menu.

Insert Image

Up One Level

2 On the toolbar, click Edit.

The FrontPage Express window opens.

3 On the Ferguson and Bardell page, scroll down until you see the second paragraph of text.

4 Position the insertion point at the end of the first paragraph, and press ENTER.

5 On the Formatting toolbar, click the Insert Image button.

The Image dialog box appears with the From File option selected.

6 In the From File area, click Browse.

The Image dialog box appears.

7 In the Image dialog box, click the Up One Level button until the c:\ drive is displayed.

8 Double-click the Internet Explorer 4 SBS Practice folder.

9 Click the new.jpg file, and then click Open.

The New button is placed at the insertion point on the page.

Insert text

In this exercise, you insert a heading next to the New button.

1 At the insertion point, type **Intranet Services Department to be launched this fall!** and press ENTER.

The heading is added to the page. The text must be reformatted to increase the font size and make the heading bold.

2 Select the text "Intranet Services Department to be launched this fall!"

3 On the Formatting toolbar, click the Increase Text Size button.

The font size is increased.

Increase Text Size

You can also reformat text by selecting Font on the Format menu.

4 On the Formatting toolbar, click the Bold button.

5 Click anywhere on the page.

The text is no longer selected. Your screen should look similar to the following illustration.

Bold

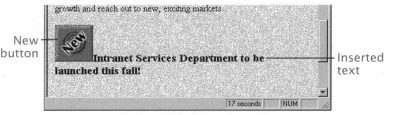

Change the image properties

In this exercise, you change the amount of space between the New button and the text.

For a demonstration of how to change the image properties refer tp p.xxii in the Using the Microsoft Internet Explorer 4 Step by Step CD-ROM section.

1 Right-click the New button.

   A shortcut menu is displayed.

2 On the shortcut menu, click Image Properties.

   The Image Properties dialog box appears, with the General tab selected.

3 In the Image Properties dialog box, click the Appearance tab.

4 In the Layout area, click the Alignment down arrow, and select absmiddle.

   You can specify how text will be aligned around the button by using the Alignment menu choices. The absmiddle option aligns the middle of the image with the middle of the largest item in the text line. This should be used when you have a short line of text, such as a heading, that you want to place next to a graphic.

5 In the Layout area, click the Horizontal Spacing up arrow until the number reaches 15 or type in **15**.

   The Horizontal Spacing option is used to insert space between the button and the text. In the Horizontal Spacing box, the greater the number, the larger the space between the graphic and the text.

6 Click OK.

Save the file

In this exercise, you save the Western Division page you have just edited to your disk.

1 On the File menu, click Save As.

2 In the Save As dialog box, click As File.

3 In the Save In box, be sure that Internet Explorer 4 SBS Practice is displayed.

4 Click Save.

   The file is saved in your Practice folder. You do not need to save the New button to your disk because the button is already in your Practice folder. If you had edited a page that was not included in these lessons, you would have to save each graphics file.

5 In the replace existing file box, click Yes.

Publishing Pages on the Web

When you are finished editing a Web page, you can save it to your computer or publish it on the Web. The page is not accessible to others until you publish it to a *Web server*, which is a computer that holds Web pages and is connected to the Internet or to your company's intranet.

A Web Publishing Wizard is included with Internet Explorer to make it easy for you to upload all of your HTML pages and graphics files to a server. You can use the wizard from within FrontPage Express, by clicking the Save button on the Standard toolbar, by selecting Save or Save As on the File menu, or from the Desktop, by clicking the Start button, pointing to Programs, pointing to Internet Explorer, and then selecting Web Publishing Wizard. To complete all of the screens included with the wizard, you need the information provided by your Internet Service Provider, or your network administrator, on how to publish pages to the Web.

Creating a Personal Web Page

Creating a Web page is a quick way to relay information to many people at once. With FrontPage Express, you can create your own Web page by using a Personal Home Page Wizard to guide you through the steps. After you construct the page using the wizard, you can go back anytime and fill in more text or graphics on the page.

 WEB PICK   Interested in pursuing a career in Web page creation or design? Check out the HTML Writers Guild at http://www.hwg.org

At Ferguson and Bardell, you decide that publishing a personal Web page would be a good way to introduce yourself to others in the company.

Create a personal Web page

In this exercise, you create a new Web page using the Personal Home Page Wizard.

1   On the File menu, click New.

The New Page dialog box appears.

2   In the Template Or Wizard area, click Personal Home Page Wizard, and click OK.

3 In the Select The Major Sections For Your Home Page area, make sure that only the following are selected:

Employee Information

Current Projects

Contact Information

4 Click Next.

The progress bar at the bottom of the screen tells you how far along you are in the Web page creation process. Your screen should look similar to the following illustration.

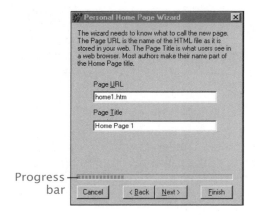

Progress bar

5 In the Page URL area, type **Mypage.htm,** and then press TAB.

You will save your personal Web page to your computer during this exercise. If you were publishing the page to the Web, you would type the URL assigned to your page in the Page URL area.

6 In the Page Title area, type **Systems Coordinator**, and then click Next.

7 In the Select The Information To Include In This Section area, make sure only the following are selected:

Key Responsibilities

Department Or Workgroup

8 Click Next.

9 In the Current Project box, type **Establishing an Intranet Services Department**, and press ENTER. Type **Compiling intranet resources list**, be sure that the Bullet List check box is selected, and then click Next.

10 Leave the Contact Information as is, and then click Next.

11 In the Home Page Sections area, click Current Projects, and then click Up twice.

Current Projects is listed at the top of the list.

12 Click Next, and then click Finish.

The page is displayed. Your screen should look similar to the following illustration.

Personal web page

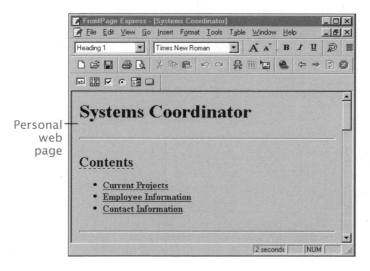

Save

13 On the toolbar, click the Save button.

The Save As dialog box appears.

14 In the Save As dialog box, click As File.

15 In the Save In box, be sure that Internet Explorer 4 SBS Practice is displayed.

When you finish Step 16, leave files open. You will close them in the "Finish the lesson" exercise later in this lesson.

16 In the Save As File dialog box, click Save.

The file is saved to your computer.

NOTE If you'd like to build on the skills that you learned in this lesson, you can work through the exercises in One Step Further. Otherwise, skip to "Finish the lesson."

One Step Further: Viewing Folders as Web Pages

You can customize your folders with the same HTML codes used to construct Web pages. That way, when you open the folder, you see a full HTML page rather than just folder icons and file names. This feature is referred to as "viewing the folder as a Web page" because you are using the coding language, HTML, that is used for Web pages. However, the HTML folder pages you create are stored locally and are not downloaded onto the World Wide Web.

Displaying your folders as Web pages is like creating a cover page for a folder. You can include information about the folder contents or instructions on how to use the folder items on the HTML page.

Create a new folder

In this exercise, you create a new folder.

1 On the taskbar, click the Show Desktop icon.

2 On the Desktop, click My Computer, and then click the drive where the practice files are installed.

3 On the File menu, point to New, and then click Folder.

A New Folder icon is displayed.

4 In the New Folder box, type **My Files**, and press ENTER.

The new folder is named My Files.

5 Maximize the window.

Customize a folder

In this exercise, you customize the My Files folder so it can be viewed as a Web page. To save typing time, the text of the HTML page is included in the practice files.

For a demonstration of how to customize a folder, refer to p.xxii in the Using the Microsoft Internet Explorer 4 Step by Step CD-ROM section.

IMPORTANT To complete this lesson, you must have the practice files installed on your computer. For information on how to install the practice files, see the "Installing and Using the Practice Files" section earlier in this book.

1 On your directory list, click the My Files folder.

2 On the View menu, click Customize This Folder.

3 In the What Would You Like To Do? area, select the Choose A Background Picture option, and then click Next.

TIP Some items on the Desktop, such as My Computer and Control Panel, are already set up in the default Web view page format. If you want to see what this format looks like when it is applied to a folder, the next time you are in My Computer or Control Panel, select As Web Page on the View menu.

4 In the Customize This Folder dialog box, click Browse.

5 Click the Look In down arrow, and then select the SBS Practice File folder on the C drive.

6 Click the Files of Type down arrow, and then choose GIF.

7 In the Open dialog box, double-click world.gif .

8 Click Next, and then click Finish.

The My Files folder is displayed as a Web page. Your screen should look similar to the following illustration.

Folder viewed as Web page

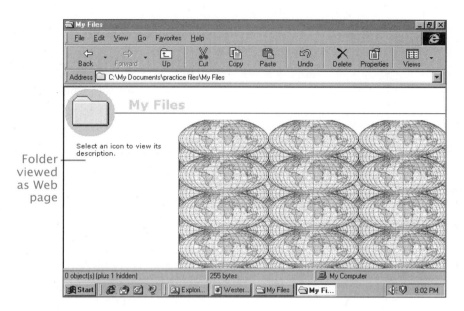

 NOTE The FOLDER.HTM and DESKTOP.INI files are added when you customize a folder. These files are required to view the folder as a Web page. Do not delete these files.

View a folder

You can also click As Web Page on the View menu.

If you did not complete the One Step Further exercises, skip steps 1 through 4.

You can view a folder with or without the Web page displayed. In this exercise, you learn how to stop and start viewing a folder as a Web page.

1 On the toolbar, click the Views down arrow.

The Views menu is displayed.

2 On the Views menu, click As Web Page.

The folder is no longer displayed as a Web page.

3 On the toolbar, click the Views down arrow.

4 On the Views menu, click As Web Page.

The folder is displayed as a Web page again.

Finish the lesson

In this exercise, you delete the folder you created and customized to view as a Web page, exit FrontPage Express, and exit Internet Explorer.

1 On the taskbar, click the Show Desktop icon.

2 On the Desktop, click My Computer, and then click the drive where the practice files are installed.

3 On the directory list, right-click the My Files folder.

4 On the shortcut menu, click Delete.

5 In the Confirm Folder Delete dialog box, click Yes.

6 On the taskbar, click the FrontPage Express button.

7 In FrontPage Express, on the File menu, click Exit.

8 On the taskbar, click the button that says Western Division.

If you are using a network connection, skip steps 10 and 11.

9 In Internet Explorer, on the File menu, click Close.

10 On the taskbar, right-click your modem icon.

11 Click Sign Out, and then click yes.

Lesson Summary

To	Do this	Button
Print a selected frame	Select text within the frame you want to print. On the File menu, click Print. In the Print Frames area, select Only The Selected Frame, and click OK.	
Print frames individually	On the File menu, click Print. In the Print Frames area, select All Frames Individually, and click OK.	
Print a list of linked pages	On the File menu, click Print. Select Print Table Of Links, and click OK.	
Print the entire page, how it appears on the screen	On the File menu, click Print. In the Print Frames area, select As Laid Out On Screen, and click OK.	
Print from the toolbar	On the toolbar, click Print.	
Save a Web page	On the File menu, click Save As. In the Save HTML Document dialog box, click the Save In down arrow, select the drive or folder, and click OK.	

To	Do this	Button
Save a graphic	Right-click the graphic. On the shortcut menu, click Save Picture As. In the Save Picture dialog box, select a drive or folder, and then click Save.	
Save the background	Right-click the background. On the shortcut menu, click Save Background As. In the Save Picture dialog box, select the drive or folder, and then click Save.	
View a saved page from your computer	On the Address bar, type the file name, and press ENTER.	
Insert a graphics file on a Web page	On the toolbar, click Edit. In FrontPage Express, on the toolbar, click Insert Image. In the From File area, click Browse. In the Image dialog box, click the Look In up arrow, and select a drive or folder. Select the file, and then click Open.	
Insert text by a graphic	Next to the graphic, type the text, and press ENTER.	
Reformat the text by a graphic	Select the text. On the Formatting toolbar, click the Increase Text Size button, and then click the Bold button.	
Change image properties	Right-click the image. On the shortcut menu, click Image Properties. In the Image Properties dialog box, click the Appearance tab. In the Layout area, click the Horizontal Spacing up arrow until the number reaches the desired spacing.	
Save an edited Web page to disk	On the File menu, click Save As. In the Save As dialog box, select your practice folder, and then click Save.	

To	Do this	Button
Create a personal Web page	On the File menu, click New. In the Template Or Wizard area, click Personal Home Page Wizard, and click OK. Make your selections on each page, and click Next. On the final page, click Finish. On the toolbar, click the Save button. In the Save As dialog box, click As File. In the Save As File dialog box, select your practice folder, and then click Save.	

For online information about	On the Help menu, click Contents And Index, click the Index tab, and then type
Printing frames, and printing Web pages	**printing Web pages**
Saving Web pages to disk	**saving information from Web pages**
Editing Web pages (in FrontPage Express help file)	**editing Web pages**
Creating your own Web page in FrontPage Express (in Front Page Express help file)	**creating Web pages**

Review & Practice

Estimated time
20 min.

- Add a Web page to the Desktop.
- Subscribe to a channel.
- Add a Web page to your Favorites list and subscribe to the page.
- Edit a Web page.
- Create a personal Web page.

Before you move on to Part 3, which covers sending and receiving e-mail, posting messages in newsgroups, and meeting with people over the Internet, you can practice the skills you learned in Part 2 by working through this Review & Practice section. You will add a Web page to your Desktop, subscribe to a channel from the Channel Guide, and add a subscription to a page on your Favorites list. You will also edit a Web page in FrontPage Express and create a personal Web page.

Scenario

As systems coordinator at Ferguson and Bardell, you set up PCs for new employees. A new vice president of Finance has just been hired, and you need to set up a PC that displays business news on the Desktop. You also need to enter subscriptions to financial news services on the PC. It's also your job to update the Ferguson and Bardell Employee Profiles page on the company intranet to include the new employees and create a personal Web page to introduce the new employees to the rest of the company.

Step 1: Add a Web Page to the Desktop

To customize the Desktop on the new vice president's PC, you add the business section from an online newspaper to the Desktop.

1 Start Internet Explorer.
2 Go to the Desktop.
3 Be sure that the Desktop is being viewed as a Web page.
4 Add the http://www.usatoday.com/money/mfront.htm page to the Desktop.
5 On the Desktop, resize the Web page.

For more information about	See
Going to the Desktop from Internet Explorer	Lesson 4
Displaying a Web page on the Desktop	Lesson 4
Resizing a Web page on the Desktop	Lesson 4

Step 2: Subscribe to a Channel

It is company policy to supply the Wall Street Journal to all executives. You set up a channel subscription to the Wall Street Journal and manually update the subscription so the content is available immediately for offline reading.

1 Preview the available channels in the Channel Guide.
2 In the Business category of the Channel Guide, view the Wall Street Journal page.
3 Subscribe to the Wall Street Journal channel.
4 Manually update the Wall Street Journal page.

For more information about	See
Previewing channels in the Channel Guide	Lesson 4
Subscribing to a channel	Lesson 4
Updating a subscription manually	Lesson 4

Step 3: Add a Web Page to the List of Favorites and Subscribe to the Page

In your Web-browsing experience, you have accumulated a list of Web sites related to financial news. You add a financial news page to the Favorites list

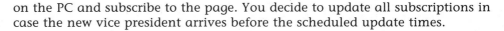

on the PC and subscribe to the page. You decide to update all subscriptions in case the new vice president arrives before the scheduled update times.

1 Go to Internet Explorer.

2 Add the http://cnnfn.com page to the Favorites list, and subscribe to the page.

3 Update all subscriptions manually.

For more information about	See
Subscribing to a page on your Favorites list	Lesson 4
Updating all subscriptions	Lesson 4

Step 4: Edit a Web Page

All employees are included on the Employee Profiles Web page. You edit the page to add the new vice president.

IMPORTANT To complete this step, you must have the practice files installed. For more information, see the "Installing and Using the Practice Files" section earlier in this book.

1 In Internet Explorer, open the Profiles.htm page. (Hint: To open the file, type the full path name on the Address bar.)

2 Edit the page to include an entry about Mary Tanner. At the bottom of the page, add Mary Tanner as a heading. Increase the text size of the heading, and make the heading bold.

3 Below the heading, type **In her free time, Mary enjoys sailing and scuba diving.**

4 Save the file to disk.

For more information about	See
Editing a Web page in FrontPage Express	Lesson 5
Saving an HTML page to disk in FrontPage Express	Lesson 5

Step 5: Create a Personal Web Page

Every employee has a personal Web page on the Ferguson and Bardell intranet. To help your new vice president get her Web page up and running, you create a basic personal Web page that she can fill in later.

1   In FrontPage Express, create a new Web page using the Personal Home Page Wizard. (Hint: On the File menu, click New, click Personal Home Page Wizard, and click OK.)

2   Include the following information on the Web page.

Sections: Employee Information, Personal Interests, Contact Information

Page URL: MaryT.htm

Page Title: Mary Tanner

Employee Information Section: Job Title

Personal Interests: Sailing and Scuba Diving. Display the personal interests in a bullet list.

E-mail address: maryt@wideworldimporters.com

3   Save the page in your practice folder with the file name MaryT.htm.

4   Exit FrontPage Express.

For more information about	See
Creating a personal Web page in FrontPage Express	Lesson 5
Saving a personal Web page	Lesson 5

Finish the Review & Practice

Follow these steps to delete the subscriptions you created in this Review & Practice, and then quit Internet Explorer.

1   On the Desktop, delete the USA Today Web page and the subscription to the page.

2   On the Channels Bar, delete the Wall Street Journal folder and the subscription.

3   In Internet Explorer, delete the Cnnfn subscription.

4   If you want to continue to the next lesson, on the Standard toolbar, click Home.

5   If you are finished using Internet Explorer for now, on the File menu, click Close.

6   In the Disconnect dialog box, click Yes.

7   In the Reconnect dialog box, click No.

Part 2

Communicating on the Internet

Using E-mail

Estimated time
25 min.

In this lesson you will learn how to:

■ Create and send messages.

■ Read messages in your Inbox.

■ Reply to messages and forward messages.

■ Update your Address Book.

■ Find people on the Internet.

Electronic mail (e-mail) is the most popular form of communication on the Internet. It is a fast and economical way for anyone with a PC and modem to keep in touch with business associates, friends, and family members. E-mail allows you to combine the clarity of a written letter with the immediacy of a phone call. You can use e-mail at your job to communicate with other employees or in your personal life to stay up-to-date with friends and relatives around the world.

The Outlook Express program manages your Internet e-mail and newsgroup messages. In Outlook Express, you can write messages on stationery, send and receive file attachments, and even send a Web page.

If you don't know the e-mail address of a person or business on the Internet, you can use directories in Outlook Express to find people on the Internet. As you send and receive messages, you can build a personal online Address Book of the e-mail addresses you use the most.

In your role as sales manager at Wide World Importers, you must stay in close contact with your sales representatives in stores across the country. You use e-mail to manage your sales team, send corporate announcements, share monthly sales reports, and maintain daily contact with the members of your team via e-mail.

Start Outlook Express

In this exercise, you start Outlook Express from your Desktop.

IMPORTANT   To complete this lesson, you must have your mail account established in Outlook Express. For information on how to set up your mail account, see Appendix A.

Launch Outlook Express

If you are using a network connection, skip steps 2 and 3.

If you did not disconnect from the Internet after the previous lesson, you can skip steps 2 and 3. In the Outlook Express dialog box, click Cancel.

1   On the taskbar, click the Launch Outlook Express icon.

Outlook Express opens.

2   In the Outlook Express dialog box, click the Select The Connection You Would Like To Dial down arrow, click your Internet Service Provider connection, and click OK.

3   In the Connect To dialog box, type your password, and click OK.

The Outlook Express screen with the contents of the Outlook Express folder is displayed. Your screen should look similar to the following illustration. If necessary, maximize the screen.

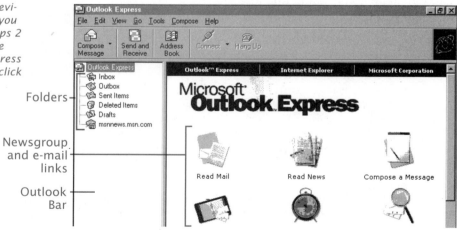

Folders

Newsgroup and e-mail links

Outlook Bar

You'll learn more about the news server in Lesson 7.

E-mail is organized in folders in Outlook Express. The folders are displayed on the Outlook Bar along with an icon you can use to connect to your news server. The following table describes the folders you see on the Outlook Bar.

This folder	Is used to
Inbox	Store e-mail messages you receive.
Outbox	Hold e-mail messages that are ready to be sent.
Sent Items	Keep copies of messages you have sent.
Deleted Items	Provide a temporary storage area for messages you have deleted.
Drafts	Hold messages you are not finished writing.

Composing and Sending Messages

You can compose e-mail messages while you are online or offline. If you compose online, the message is sent when you click the Send button; if you compose offline, the message is stored in your Outbox until you go online and send it.

For a demonstration of how to compose a message, refer to p.xxii in the Using the Microsoft Internet Explorer 4 Step by Step CD-ROM section.

Like the rest of the Internet, e-mail has come a long way in a short period of time. In the past, only plain text messages could be sent via e-mail. Now, you can apply formatting to text to emphasize words in bold, create indented lists, and even send your message on stationery. If you have Microsoft Office 95, Microsoft Office 97, or Microsoft Word on your PC, you can use the spell checker from one of these programs to check spelling in your e-mail message.

Compose a message

In this exercise, you write an e-mail message and format the text in the message.

1 On the toolbar, click Compose Message.

The New Message dialog box appears.

2 In the To box, type your e-mail address.

You can also click New Message on the Compose menu.

NOTE Normally, you would not send a message to yourself. However, for the purposes of this lesson, you will send e-mail to yourself, and then open the messages in your Inbox.

You will learn how to use the Address Book later in this lesson.

3 Click in the Subject area, and type **Quarterly Meeting**

4   In the Message area, type **The quarterly meeting will be held in Seattle, September 10-12.**

Font size

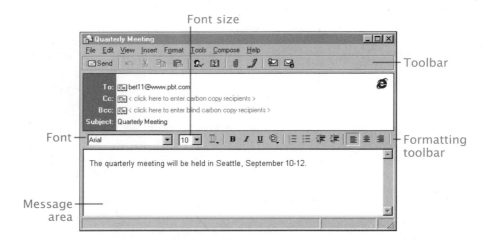

Toolbar

Font

Formatting toolbar

Message area

5   In the Message area, select the text you just typed.

6   On the Formatting toolbar, click the Font Size down arrow, and then click 12.

The font size is increased. You can use the buttons on the Formatting toolbar to change the appearance of text in your message.

7   On the toolbar, click the Send button.

The Send Mail dialog box is displayed.

8   Click the Don't Show Me This Message Again box, and then click OK.

TIP   If you would rather send the message at a later time, on the File menu, click Send Later, and the message will be stored in your Outbox. If you would rather store the message in your Drafts folder instead of sending it, on the File menu, click Save.

Sent Items

9   On the Outlook Bar, click Sent Items.

The message you just sent is displayed.

Compose a message using stationery

You can compose e-mail messages on a variety of stationery designs in Outlook Express. For example, there are birthday or holiday designs for special occasions and more formal designs for business use. In this exercise, you write an e-mail message on stationery in Outlook Express.

TIP To preview the stationery provided in Outlook Express, on the Tools menu, click Stationery, and then click the Mail tab. Select the This Stationery check box, and then click Select. The stationery designs are displayed in a Preview area.

1   On the toolbar, click the Compose Message down arrow, and then click Formal Announcement.

   The formal announcement stationery is displayed in the Message area.

2   Maximize the New Message window so that you can see all of the stationery page.

3   In the To box, type your e-mail address.

 TIP To send a copy of the message to another recipient, type the recipient's e-mail address in the Cc box. To send a blind carbon copy to another recipient, type the recipient's e-mail address in the Bcc box. All recipients of the message see the names in the Cc box, but only the individual recipient of the blind carbon copy sees the name in the Bcc box.

4   Click in the Subject box, and then type **Congratulations!**

5   In the Message area, select the "Your message here" text, and then type **I'm pleased to announce that Helen Morris has been promoted to Regional Sales Supervisor.**

Message on
formal
announcement
stationery

6   On the toolbar, click the Send button.

The message is sent. It is displayed in your Sent Items folder.

> **NOTE**   You might want to check with the recipient of your
> message before you send a message on stationery. Some older
> e-mail systems might not read the stationery's design properly.

Create a signature file

In addition to using stationery, there are other ways to customize your messages. For example, you can add a signature block that lists your job title, organization, and personal Web page address. Depending on the type of messages you are sending, you might want to include your hobbies or interests. When you use a signature file, you do not have to retype your signature block on each message. You can have the signature file added automatically to each e-mail message you write. In this exercise, you create a signature file to add to the messages you send to your sales team.

1   On the Tools menu, click Stationery.

2   Be sure that the Mail tab is selected.

3   In the Signature area, click Signature.

4   In the Signature dialog box, select the Add This Signature To All Outgoing Messages check box.

If you already have your signature information stored in a file, you can select the File check box and then enter the file name.

The Don't Add Signature To Replies And Forwards check box is selected automatically when you select the Add This Signature To All Outgoing Messages check box.

5   Be sure that the Text option is selected.

6   In the Text box, type the following information.

Tom Kingston

Sales Manager

Wide World Importers

Your screen should look similar to the following illustration.

Message list

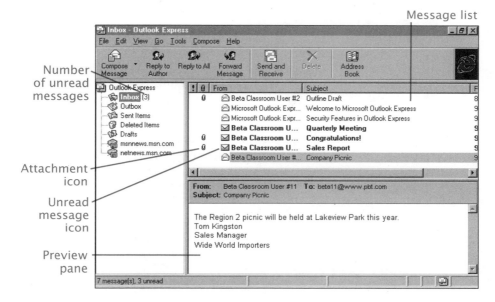

Number of unread messages

Attachment icon

Unread message icon

Preview pane

7 In the Signature dialog box, click OK.

8 Click OK.

Your signature file is added.

Digital Signatures

A *digital signature* is one component of a *digital ID*. A digital ID is similar to an electronic ID card. The digital ID is assigned to you by a certifying authority and is made up of a public key, a private key, and a digital signature. If you want to exchange *encrypted* messages with another person, you use the public key and private key. Encrypted messages are coded so other people cannot read them. You must have the key to decode and read the message. If you want the recipient to know that the message is authentic and came from you, you can digitally sign it. Digital IDs are also known as certificates.

You can obtain a digital ID by clicking Options on the Tools menu, clicking the Security tab, and then clicking the Get Digital ID button. This will connect you to the Digital ID information page at the Microsoft Web site, and from there you can use a link to get to the certifying authority's Web page.

After you have your digital ID, to add the digital signature to a message, you can click the Digitally Sign Message button on the toolbar when you compose the message.

Digitally Sign Message

Attach a file to a message

Sending files via e-mail is a great way to share information when you are working on a project or distributing information to the project team. The recipient of the file can save it to disk and then read, edit, and print the information in the original program, such as Word, Excel, or FrontPage Express. In this exercise, you write an e-mail cover letter and attach a file containing a Monthly Sales Report to the message.

 IMPORTANT To complete this lesson you will need to have the practice files installed. For more information, see the "Installing and Using the Practice Files" section in Appendix A on the CD-ROM.

1   On the toolbar, click Compose Message.

The New Message dialog box appears. Your signature file is displayed automatically because you selected the Add This Signature To All Outgoing Messages option.

2   In the To box, type your e-mail address.

3   In the Subject box, type **Sales Report**

4   In the Message area, type **Attached is the Monthly Sales Report.**

5   On the toolbar, click the Insert File button.

The Insert Attachment dialog box appears.

Insert File

You can also select File Attachment on the Insert menu.

6   In the Insert Attachment dialog box, click the Sales.htm file, and then click Attach.

The file is displayed as an attachment on the screen.

NOTE Sending compressed files speeds up transmission time. You can compress your file with commercial programs such as WinZip or PKZip that are available in computer stores or on the Web at http://www.winzip.com and http://www.pkware.com respectively.

7   On the toolbar, click the Send button.

The message is sent. It is displayed in your Sent Items folder.

Composing Messages Offline

You do not need to be connected to the Internet to compose messages. You can compose messages offline, and store the finished messages in your Outbox and the unfinished messages in your Drafts folder. Then, when you are ready to send the messages, you can connect to the Internet and send all of the finished messages from your Outbox at one time. This is a good way to conserve your time online if your connection time is limited.

Compose a message offline

In this exercise, you disconnect from the Internet and compose a message offline.

1 On the File menu, click Hang Up.

Your Internet connection is disconnected.

2 On the toolbar, click Compose Message.

The New Message dialog box appears.

3 In the To box, type your e-mail address.

 TIP You can send one message to many recipients by separating the e-mail addresses with semicolons or commas in the To box.

4 In the Subject box, type **Company Picnic**

You can check spelling in a message by selecting Spelling from the Tools menu.

5 In the Message area, type **The Region 2 picnic will be held at Lakeview Park this year.**

6 In the Company Picnic window, on the File menu, click Send Later.

A message is displayed indicating that the message will be sent the next time you click the Send And Receive button on the Outlook Express toolbar.

7 In the Send Mail dialog box, click OK.

The Company Picnic window closes.

Send messages from your Outbox

If you are using a network connection, skip steps 1 and 2.

When you use the Send And Receive button, the program delivers new mail to your Inbox and sends messages stored in your Outbox. In this exercise, you send the message stored in your Outbox using the Send And Receive button.

1 On the toolbar, click Send And Receive.

The Connect To dialog box appears.

Send and Receive

2 In the Connect To dialog box, type your password, and click OK.

You are connected to the Internet. The message in your Outbox is sent, and new mail is delivered to your Inbox. The message is removed from your Outbox and added to your Sent Items folder.

You can also click Outbox, and then select Send And Receive on the Tools menu.

Reading Messages

Messages you receive are stored in your Inbox. You can tell how many unread messages you have in your Inbox by looking at the Outlook Bar; the number of unread messages is displayed next to the Inbox label.

Your Inbox screen is divided into two parts. The upper part of the screen, called the message list, shows the subject and author of the message. The lower part of the screen, called the preview pane, shows the text of the message. You can scan the message list to determine which messages you want to read.

Receive new mail

In this exercise, you receive new mail and read your incoming messages.

Inbox

If you would rather read the message in a larger window, on the message list, double-click the message. A new message window opens, and you can see more text at one time than you can see in the preview pane.

1   On the Outlook Bar, click Inbox.

   Your Inbox opens, and your new messages are displayed.

2   On the message list, click the Company Picnic message.

   The text of the message is displayed in the preview pane.

Read an attachment to a message

In this exercise, you view the messages in your Inbox and read a file attached to a message.

1   In the message list, right-click the Attachment icon on the Sales Report message.

   A shortcut menu is displayed.

2   On the shortcut menu, click Open.

   The message is displayed in a New Message window.

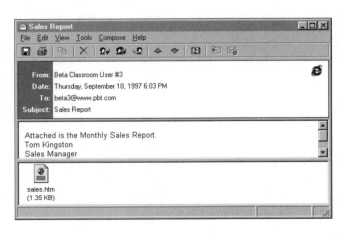

Attachment

3 In the New Message window, right-click the Sales.htm attachment.

A shortcut menu is displayed.

4 On the shortcut menu, click Open, select the Open It option and click OK.

> **TIP** If you want to save an attached file to your disk, you can use the Save As option on the shortcut menu.

5 Close the Internet Explorer window.

6 Close the New Message window.

Set up the Inbox Assistant to handle messages automatically

The Inbox Assistant is available to help you manage your e-mail messages. In this exercise, you set up the Inbox Assistant so that all of your Quarterly Meeting messages are copied automatically to the Meetings folder.

1 On the Tools menu, click Inbox Assistant.

2 In the Inbox Assistant dialog box, click Add.

The Properties dialog box appears.

3 In the When A Message Arrives With The Following Criteria area, in the Subject box, type **Quarterly Meeting**

4 In the Perform The Following Action area, select the Copy To check box, and then click Folder.

The Copy dialog box appears.

5 In the Copy dialog box, click New Folder.

6 In the Folder Name box, type **Meetings**, and click OK.

7 In the Copy dialog box, click Meetings, and click OK.

Meetings is displayed in the Copy To box.

8 On the Properties dialog box, click OK.

9 In the Inbox Assistant dialog box, click OK.

Responding to a Message

Outlook Express gives you several options for responding to the e-mail messages you receive. You can compose a new message from scratch or directly reply to the author of a sent message. When you respond to a message, you can send your reply to the sender of the message only or to all recipients of the original message. You can include the document you received as well as your response in your reply. You can also forward messages to a third party.

Reply to a message

In this exercise, you write a response to a message you have received and send the response to the author of the message.

 TIP You can automatically add to your Address Book the e-mail address of the person to whom you are replying. On the Tools menu, select Options, and then select the Automatically Put People I Reply To In My Address Book check box.

If you want to reply to all recipients of the message, you can click the Reply To All button.

1   In the message list, click the Quarterly Meeting message.

2   On the toolbar, click Reply To Author.

The Re: Quarterly Meeting window opens, with the original message quoted in the Message area.

3   In the Message area, type **Do you have information about hotel accommodations?**

4   On the toolbar, click Send.

The reply is sent, and the Re: Quarterly Meeting window closes.

Forward a message

In this exercise, you forward a message to a new recipient.

1   In the message list, click the Congratulations! message.

2   On the toolbar, click Forward Message.

The Fw: Congratulations! window.

3   In the To box, type your e-mail address.

You can also click Forward on the Compose menu.

 TIP You can add e-mail addresses to your Address Book from messages you receive. In the To, Cc, or Bcc box on the message screen, right-click the name, and then click Add To Address Book.

4 On the toolbar, click Send.

The reply is sent, and the Fw: Congratulations! window closes.

Printing Messages

For more infor-
mation about
printing options,
see the "Printing
a Web Page"
section in
Lesson 5.

You can print messages from any folder in Outlook Express. The print options available for printing Web pages in Internet Explorer apply when you print e-mail messages as well. For example, if links to Web sites are included in the text of the message, you can print the text of all documents linked to the message or generate a list of links contained in the message.

Print a message

In this exercise, you print the Welcome To Microsoft Outlook Express message.

1 In the message list, click the Welcome To Microsoft Outlook Express message.

You can also
right-click the
message, and
then click Print.

2 On the File menu, click Print.

The Print dialog box opens.

3 On the Print dialog box, click OK.

The message is printed.

Updating Your Address Book

Just as you keep an address book for the postal mail you send, you can create an address book to keep track of your e-mail contacts. Your Address Book acts as an online organizer that contains home addresses, business addresses, Internet conferencing, and digital IDs for business associates, colleagues, family, and friends. In your Address Book, you can organize addresses into groups that you can use like mailing lists. When you want to send a message to everyone in the group, you can type in one group name instead of individual e-mail addresses.

As your Address Book grows, you'll find that you rarely have to type e-mail addresses manually when you compose a new message. You can type in a contact's name and the e-mail address is automatically filled in.

Add a new address entry

In this exercise, you add your e-mail address to the Address Book.

Address
Book

1 On the toolbar, click Address Book.

The Address Book window opens.

New Contact

2 On the toolbar, click New Contact.

The Properties dialog box appears.

3   In the Name area, type your first name and last name.

Your full name is added automatically to the Display Name box. The Display Name is the name displayed in the Address Book window.

4   In the Add New box, type your e-mail address, and click Add.

Your e-mail address is added.

NOTE   If you are not sure if the recipient's mail program can read HTML pages or stationery, select the Send E-mail Using Plain Text Only check box.

5   On the Properties dialog box, click OK.

Create a new group

In this exercise, you create a new group and add your e-mail address to the group.

1   On the Address Book toolbar, click New Group.

2   In the Group Name box, type **Sales Contacts**

3   In the Members area, click Select Members.

The Select Group Members dialog box appears.

4   In the left pane, click your e-mail address, and then click Select.

Your e-mail address is added to the Members box.

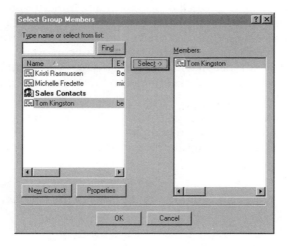

5   In the Select Group Members dialog box, click OK.

6   In the Sales Contacts Properties dialog box, click OK.

The Address Book window is displayed.

7   Minimize the Address Book window.

TIP   To see a list of the members of the group in the Address Book window, position the mouse pointer on the New Group icon. The display names and e-mail addresses of members are displayed in a ToolTip.

Send a message to a group

In this exercise, you send a message to the Sales Contacts group.

Compose Message

Select Recipients

1   On the toolbar, click Compose Message.

The New Message dialog box opens.

2   On the toolbar, click Select Recipients.

The Select Recipients dialog box opens.

3   In the left pane, click Sales Contacts, and then click To.

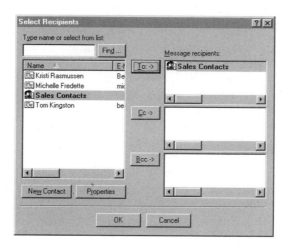

4   Click OK.

5   In the Subject box, type **Marketing Seminar**

6   In the Message area, type **Are you attending the Marketing Seminar in Dallas next month?**

Send

7   On the toolbar, click Send.

The message is sent to all e-mail addresses in the group.

Finding People on the Internet

The World Wide Web stores a number of directories you can use to look for a person's e-mail address or to locate a Web page for a business. You can select a directory from within Outlook Express or from the Start menu on the Desktop.

Locate an e-mail address in a directory

In this exercise, you look up your own name in an Internet directory.

1 Restore the Address Book window. On the Edit menu, click Find.
   The Find People dialog box appears.
2 Click the Look In down arrow and then click SwitchBoard.
3 In the Name box, type your name.
4 In the Find People dialog box, click Find Now.
   The results are displayed. If the results are not what you expected, you can try a different directory.
5 On the Find People dialog box, click Close.
6 Close the Address Book window.

NOTE If you'd like to build on the skills that you learned in this lesson, you can work through the exercises in One Step Further. Otherwise, skip to "Finish the lesson."

One Step Further: Sending Web Pages

You can send and receive messages in HTML format such as HTML pages you create and want others to review before they're posted on the Web, or Web pages you want to share with others.

NOTE The ability to share information is one of the great benefits of the Web. Remember that Web page content is copyrighted, and you should not use any elements on the page for your own use unless you have the permission of the page owner.

Send a Web page from Internet Explorer

If you do not know the URL of a Web page, you can access Internet Explorer, locate the page, and then send it. In this exercise, you send a Web page from Internet Explorer to your e-mail address.

1 On the taskbar, click the Launch Internet Explorer icon.

The Internet Explorer window opens.

2 Browse the Web until you find a page you want to send, or open one of your Favorites or History pages.

3 On the File menu, point to Send, and then click Page By E-mail.

The New Message dialog box opens.

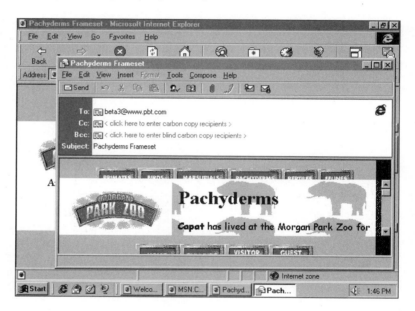

4 In the To box, type your e-mail address.
5 On the toolbar, click Send.
6 Close the Internet Explorer window.
7 On the Outlook Express toolbar, click Send And Receive.

The message is delivered to your Inbox.

Finish the lesson

If you are using a network connection, skip step 1.

In this exercise, you delete the messages you sent during this lesson and the Meetings folder you created.

1 In Outlook Express, on the File menu, click Hang Up.

2   On the Outlook Bar, click Inbox.

3   Select all files in the Inbox, and then click Delete.

4   Click the Sent Items folder, select all messages, and then click Delete.

5   Right-click the Meetings folder, and then click Delete.

6   In the Outlook Express dialog box, click Yes to confirm you want to delete the folder.

7   To continue on to the next lesson, on the Outlook Bar, click Outlook Express.

8   If you are finished using Outlook Express for now, on the File menu, click Exit.

Lesson Summary

To	Do this	Button
Start Outlook Express	On the taskbar, click Launch Outlook Express.	Compose Message
Compose a message	On the toolbar, click Compose Message. In the To box, type the recipient's e-mail address. In the Subject box, type the subject of the message. In the Message area, type the message. On the toolbar, click the Send button.	Send
Compose a message with stationery	Click the Compose Message down arrow, and then click Formal Announcement. In the To box, type the recipient's e-mail address. In the Subject box, type the subject of the message. In the Message area, type the message. On the toolbar, click the Send button.	
Create a signature file	On the Tools menu, click Stationery, click Signature, and then select the Add This Signature To All Outgoing Messages check box. In the Text box, type the information you want in your signature file. Click OK until the dialog boxes are closed.	

To	Do this	Button
Attach a file to a message	On the toolbar, click Compose Message. In the To box, type the recipient's e-mail address. In the Subject box, type the subject of the message. In the Message area, type the message. On the toolbar, click the Insert File button. In the Insert Attachment dialog box, click the file name, and then click Attach. On the toolbar, click the Send button.	
Compose a message offline	On the File menu, click Hang Up. On the toolbar, click Compose Message. In the To box, type the recipient's e-mail address. In the Subject box, type the subject of the message. In the Message area, type the message. On the File menu, click Send Later. In the Send Mail dialog box, click OK.	
Send offline messages	On the toolbar, click Send And Receive. In the Connect To dialog box, type your password, and click OK.	
Read a message and save the attachment	On the Outlook Bar, click Inbox. In the message list, select the message. Right-click the attachment icon in the preview pane. On the shortcut menu, click the file name. In the Save Attachment As dialog box, click Save.	
Set up the Inbox Assistant	On the Tools menu, click Inbox Assistant, and then click Add. In the Subject box, type the subject you want to select. Select the Copy To check box, and then click Folder. Click New Folder, type the new folder name, and click OK. In the Copy dialog box, select the folder you just created, and click OK. Click OK until all dialog boxes are closed.	

To	Do this	Button
Reply to a message	In the message list, select the message. On the toolbar, click Reply To Author. In the Message area, type the message. On the toolbar, click Send.	Reply to Author
Forward a message	In the message list, select the message. On the toolbar, click Forward. In the To box, type the recipient's e-mail address. On the toolbar, click Send.	Forward Message
Print a message	In the message list, select the message. On the File menu, click Print, and click OK.	
Add a new address entry	On the toolbar, click Address Book. On the toolbar, click New Contact. In the Name box, type your name. In the Add New box, type the e-mail address you want to add, and then click Add. On the Properties dialog box, click OK.	Address Book
Create a new group	On the toolbar, in the Address Book click New Group. In the Group Name box, type the name of the group. In the Members area, click Select Members. In the left pane, select the e-mail address you want to add, and then click Select. Click OK until all dialog boxes are closed.	New Group
Send a message to a group	On the toolbar, click Compose Message. On the toolbar, click Select Recipients. In the left pane, click the group you want to add, and then click To. Click OK. In the Subject box, type the subject of the message. In the Message area, type the message. On the toolbar, click Send.	

To	Do this
Find people on the Internet	On the Edit menu, click Find. In the Search box, select a directory. In the Name box, type the name you want to locate, and then click Find Now. On the Find People dialog box, click Close. Close the Address Book window.

For online information about	On the Help menu, click Contents And Index, click the Index tab, and then type
Sending messages	**sending mail messages**
Attaching files to messages	**sending file attachments**
Responding to messages	**mail messages**
Updating your Address Book	**address book**

Discussing Topics in Newsgroups

Estimated time
30 min.

In this lesson you will learn how to:

- Subscribe to newsgroups.
- Read newsgroup messages.
- Print and save messages.
- Contribute messages to a newsgroup discussion and send a private reply to the author of a message.
- Post a new message to a newsgroup.

The tens of thousands of newsgroups that exist on the Internet provide access to information, discussion, and instruction on nearly every conceivable topic. You can use newsgroups to debate proposed laws, discuss health issues with experts, mourn the passing of public figures, and argue the plays of your favorite sports teams. You can find new recipes, gardening tips, and solutions to computer problems.

Each newsgroup is devoted to a specific subject. When you post a message to a newsgroup, anyone who accesses the newsgroup can see your message and respond to it. A response can be posted to the newsgroup or sent privately to you at your e-mail address. Most newsgroups are open to anyone who wants to post a message. However, some newsgroups are *moderated*, which means that one or more volunteers screen messages to ensure that the messages are on-topic and appropriate for the newsgroup.

The messages you post are stored on a *news server*, which is simply a computer dedicated to the storage of newsgroups. Since the thousands of news servers around the world are connected to each other, newsgroups offer a wealth of worldwide contributions. If you are using a dial-up connection, the name of your news server was added when you set up your news account. You can also add a news server from within Outlook Express.

 WEB PICK   Want to read a newsgroup that's not available from your news server? Visit the DejaNews Web site at http://www.dejanews.com

As the new regional sales supervisor at Wide World Importers, it is important for you to keep the rest of the company informed about the events in your region through the region's Web page. You learn to use newsgroups for research purposes.

Start Outlook Express

In this exercise, you start Outlook Express from your Desktop.

 IMPORTANT   To complete the exercises in this lesson, you must have your news account established. For more information, see the "Setting Up Mail and News Accounts" section of Appendix A on the CD-ROM.

1   On the taskbar, click the Launch Outlook Express icon.

2   Log on to your Internet Service Provider using your user name and password.

Subscribing to Newsgroups

Each news server contains thousands of newsgroups. Subscribing to a newsgroup makes it easy for you to access only the newsgroups that interest you.

 NOTE   Subscribing to newsgroups does not involve money and is not related to the site or channel subscriptions you learned about in Lesson 4. Subscribing to newsgroups helps you avoid searching through all of the newsgroups on a news server to find the information you need.

To find newsgroups of interest, you can search for a specific word in the newsgroup name. For example, if you are looking for newsgroups about creating Web pages, you can search for newsgroups with "Web" or "HTML" in the newsgroup name or search in the category "comp" (computers).

The abbreviation for the category is displayed in the newsgroup name. The following table describes common categories used in newsgroup names.

Abbreviation	Category	Includes
alt	Alternative	Subjects covering anything and everything. This category has evolved into the area where you are most likely to find the widest variety of subjects, some of which you might find objectionable.
biz	Business	Business-related subjects.
comp	Computers	Subjects for every level of computer user.
misc	Miscellaneous	Varied subjects that do not fit in other categories.
news	News	General subjects about how to use newsgroups; suggested subjects for new newsgroups.
rec	Recreational	Recreational activities and hobbies.
sci	Scientific	Subjects related to science and research.
soc	Social	Subjects about social and cultural issues.

Not all newsgroup names begin with a category. You might also find some names that begin with the news server, the college that hosts the newsgroup, or the country code.

You can subscribe and unsubscribe to a newsgroup whenever you want. Unsubscribing simply removes a newsgroup from your Subscribed list, thereby removing your shortcut to that newsgroup. You can still access that newsgroup by conventional methods.

Search for words in newsgroup names

The News category has a wide variety of newsgroup listings and therefore appeals to most newsgroup readers. In this exercise, you search through news listings and subscribe to a newsgroup of your choice.

You can also click the News Server icon on the Outlook Bar.

1 On the Outlook Bar, click Outlook Express, and then click the Read News link.

The Outlook Express dialog box appears.

127

This dialog box is displayed the first time you use newsgroups because you are not subscribed to any newsgroups. It will not appear the next time you access newsgroups in Outlook Express.

2   In the Outlook Express dialog box, click Yes.

The Newsgroups dialog box appears, and the newsgroups available on your news server are displayed on the All list.

Newsgroups ⟶

Subscribed tab

3   In the Display Newsgroups Which Contain box, type **news**, but do not press ENTER.

A list of newsgroups with "news" in the name is displayed.

4   In the Newsgroups box, click a newsgroup you would like to subscribe to, and then click Subscribe.

The Newsgroups icon, which indicates that you are subscribed to the newsgroup, is displayed next to the group you have selected.

Newsgroups

5   In the Newsgroups dialog box, click the Subscribed tab.

The newsgroup you just subscribed to is displayed.

Subscribe to multiple newsgroups

If you do not know the name of a newsgroup, you can search for a specific word that you expect to appear in the newsgroup name. In this exercise, you search for newsgroups with "news" in the newsgroup name and subscribe to all of them.

1   In the Newsgroups dialog box, click the All tab.

All of the newsgroups on the news server are displayed again.

2   Be sure that News is displayed in the Display Newsgroups Which Contain box.

You might have to scroll down to select the last newsgroup.

3 In the Newsgroups box, be sure that the first newsgroup in the list is selected, press SHIFT, and then click the last newsgroup on the list.

All of the newsgroups are selected.

4 Click Subscribe.

The Newsgroups icon is displayed next to each newsgroup.

5 In the Display Newsgroups Which Contain box, select the text, and then press DELETE.

If you do not clear this box, only newsgroups with "news" in the name will be displayed in the All tab.

6 Click the Subscribed tab.

The Subscribed list is displayed.

7 In the Newsgroups dialog box, click OK.

The dialog box closes, and a list of newsgroups you subscribed to is displayed on the screen.

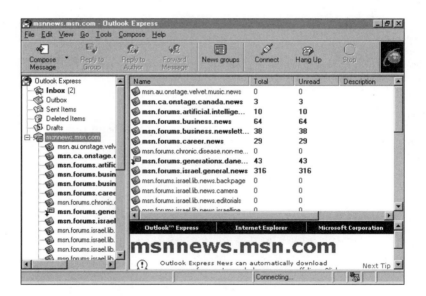

Reading Newsgroup Messages

Newsgroup messages linked together by the same topic are called *threads*. When you read newsgroup messages, you "follow a thread." Threads can have multiple levels, similar to an outline. You can expand a thread to see all replies attached to the original message or collapse a thread to see only the original message.

129

If you completed the e-mail exercises in Lesson 6, the newsgroups screen will look familiar to you. Like e-mail messages, newsgroup messages are divided into two parts, the message header and the body of the message. Message headers are displayed on the message list, and you can read the body of the message in the preview pane.

For information on how to delete message files, see the One Step Further section later in this lesson.

When you select a newsgroup to read, the messages are downloaded from the news server to your computer and stored in a *cache*. This is an area where copies of messages are stored temporarily so you can access them quickly. By default, the messages you have read are not kept in the cache, and all messages in the cache are deleted after five days. You can change these default settings or delete the message files whenever you want.

As you read newsgroup messages, the message is automatically marked as read with an icon on the message list. You can also manually mark a message as read or unread.

The following table describes the message icons you will see on the message list.

See "icons" in the Outlook Express help index for more information.

Icon name	Description
Plus	The thread is collapsed at this level. You can click this icon to expand the thread and see the replies.
Minus	The thread is expanded at this level, and you can see the replies. You can click this icon to collapse the thread.
Unread Message	The message has not been read, and the message header is bold.
Read Message	The message has been opened and is stored on your computer.
Message No Longer Available	The message is no longer available on the server.
Download	The message is tagged to be downloaded.
Download All	The messages and threads are tagged to be downloaded.
Download Without Threads	The message is tagged to be downloaded without threads.

Read messages in a newsgroup and subscribe while you are reading

You can read messages in any newsgroup on your news server. If you decide the newsgroup looks interesting, you can subscribe to it as you are reading. In this exercise, you browse through and subscribe to a newsgroup of your choice.

News groups

1   On the toolbar, click Newsgroups.

The Newsgroups dialog box appears.

2 In the Newsgroups area, be sure the All tab is selected.

All of the newsgroups available on your news server are displayed.

3 In the Display Newsgroups Which Contain box, type **events**

The newsgroups that contain "events" in the name are displayed.

You can also double-click the message to view it in a new window.

4 In the Newsgroups area, click one of the events newsgroups you are not currently subscribed to, and then click Go To.

The message headers are displayed.

5 On the Tools menu, click Subscribe To This Group.

 TIP You can resize the message list and preview pane by dragging the divider bar up or down.

News Server

6 On the Outlook Bar, click the News Server icon.

A list of subscribed newsgroups is displayed.

Read messages in a new window

You can open a new window to read messages when you want to see an attachment, or you can use the Next and Previous buttons to move through the messages. In this exercise, you read messages in the events newsgroup in a new window.

1 In the list of newsgroups, click an events newsgroup of your choice.

2 In the message list, double-click an unread message.

A new window opens. Your screen should look similar to the following illustration.

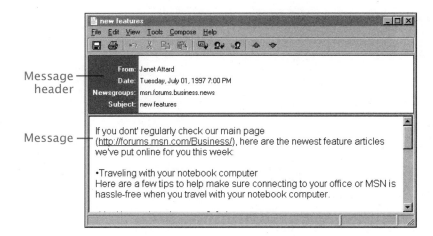

Next

Previous

3 On the toolbar, click the Next button.

The next message is displayed. You can use the Next and Previous buttons to scroll through messages quickly and in the order in which they are displayed in the message list.

4 Close the new window.

5 On the Outlook Bar, click the News Server icon.

Read messages in a thread

In this exercise, you read the message threads in the news list.

For a demonstration of how to read messages in a thread, refer to p.xxii in the Using the Microsoft Internet Explorer 4 Step by Step CD-ROM section.

If a thread is collapsed, only the main message is displayed when you click the Next and Previous buttons.

1 In the list of newsgroups, click a newsgroup of your choice.

The message headers are displayed in the message list, and the first message is displayed on the preview pane. The status bar shows the total number of messages and the number of unread messages.

2 In the message list, scroll down until you locate the main message of a thread.

The main message of a thread is indicated by the Plus icon.

3 On the main message, click the Plus icon.

The thread expands, and replies to the main message are displayed. A thread can have multiple levels, and each level can be expanded and collapsed. Your screen should look similar to the following illustration.

Plus icon —

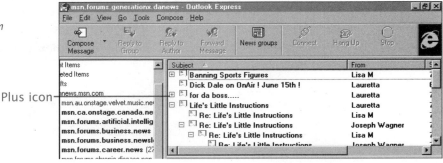

4 In the message list, click the main message.

The message is displayed in the preview pane.

5 In the message list, click the first reply.

The reply message is displayed in the preview pane.

6 In the message list, on the main message, click the Minus icon.

The thread collapses.

7 In the folder list, click the News Server icon.

The list of newsgroups you are subscribed to is displayed.

You can also click the News Server icon on the Outlook Bar to display the folder list.

Reading Messages Offline

Just as you can read e-mail offline, you can read newsgroup messages without being connected to the Internet. This is a great way to save connection time and read the newsgroup messages at your convenience.

In order to read messages offline, you must mark the desired newsgroups and then download them from the news server. When the download is finished, you can disconnect from the Internet and read the messages.

Mark a newsgroup for offline reading

When you read messages offline, you are reading from files stored on your hard drive. Messages that have not been downloaded are kept on the news-group server.

In this exercise, you mark a newsgroup of your choice for offline reading.

You can also right-click the newsgroup, click Properties or point to Mark For Retrieval on the Tools menu, and then click All Messages.

1 On the Outlook Bar, click a newsgroup of your choice.

2 On the File menu, click Properties.

3 In the Properties dialog box, click the Download tab.

4 In the Download Properties area, select the When Downloading This Newsgroup, Retrieve check box.

5 In the Download Properties area, select the All Messages (Headers And Bodies) check box.

6 In the Properties dialog box, click OK.

Download the messages for offline reading

In this exercise, you download messages in the newsgroup for offline reading.

1 On the Tools menu, click Download All.

The Outlook Express dialog box appears. You can track the progress of the messages in the dialog box if you click Details.

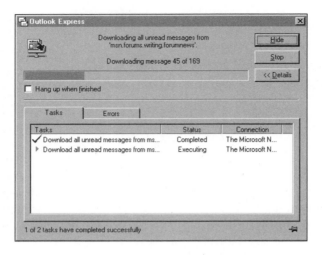

**Marked For
Download**

When the download is complete, the Marked For Download icon is
displayed next to the newsgroups you chose.

2   On the toolbar, click Hang Up.

3   Click OK. You are no longer connected.

Reading messages offline

In this exercise, you read one of the downloaded newsgroup messages offline.

*If you are using
a network
connection,
skip step 1.*

1   On the list of newsgroups you have downloaded, double-click a message
of your choice.

   TIP   You can move the preview pane so that it is displayed
beside the message list instead of below the list by clicking
Layout on the View menu and then selecting the Beside
Messages check box.

*If you are using
a network con-
nection, skip
steps 4 and 5.*

2   In the message list, click the next message you want to read.

3   Close the message window.

4   On the toolbar, click Connect.

5   If necessary, in the Connect To dialog box, type your password, and click
OK.

You are reconnected to your service provider.

6   On the Outlook Bar, click the News Server icon.

Newsgroup Terminology

The more you read newsgroups, the more likely you are to encounter terms that have a special meaning when applied to newsgroups. The following table describes these terms.

Word	Description
emoticons	"Emotion icons" that you can create using symbols on your keyboard. The most common emoticon is :) (smiley face). Also called "smileys." To see extensive lists of emoticons, the next time you are in Internet Explorer, select your favorite search engine, and search for "emoticon" or "smileys."
FAQ	A message that contains Frequently Asked Questions. Most newsgroups have a FAQ that outlines what's appropriate to post and what's not. You should read the FAQ before you post messages or replies.
flame	To criticize a message that was posted on a newsgroup. For example, if you post a message that is not appropriate for the newsgroup, you might get flamed.
lurk	To read a newsgroup without contributing messages.
post	To add a message to the newsgroup, or the message you post to a newsgroup. The message is also called an "article."
spam	To post one message to multiple newsgroups, usually to advertise a product or a "get rich quick" scheme. You can buy programs to block these types of messages.
UseNet	The term that describes all of the computers that are connected and dedicated to newsgroups.

Printing and Saving Messages

If you find a good tip or the answer to a question in a newsgroup message, you can print the message or save it to disk for future reference. As in other areas of the Internet, content in newsgroup messages is the property of the message author. You should not use the content for anything other than reference material without the permission of the author.

Print the current message

In this exercise, you print a message from a newsgroup.

IMPORTANT To complete this exercise, you must have a printer connected to your computer.

1   In the list of newsgroups you are subscribed to, click the newsgroup you want to print.

2   In the message list, click the message you want to print.

3   On the File menu, click Print.

If you do not need to select print options, in the message list, right-click the message you want to print, and then click Print. The message is printed immediately.

The Print dialog box appears.

4   In the Print dialog box, click the Number Of Copies up arrow until the number reaches 2, and click OK.

The message is printed.

NOTE If you want to print multiple messages in an adjacent range, click the first message, hold down [SHIFT], and click the last message. If you want to print nonadjacent multiple messages, click the first message, hold down [CTRL], and click the other messages. To proceed, on the File menu, click Print.

Save a message to a file on disk

In this exercise, you save a message from a newsgroup to a file on disk.

1   In the message list, click the message you want to save.

2   On the File menu, click Save As.

The Save Message As dialog box appears.

If you want to give the message a new name, type the file name in the File Name box.

3   Be sure that the file name you want is displayed in the File Name box, and then click Save.

The file is saved in the location displayed in the Save In box.

4   On the Outlook Bar, click the News Server icon.

Filtering Newsgroup Messages

Sometimes it's necessary to gain some control over an open forum. If you want to limit the number of messages you see, you can set up newsgroup filters to screen out messages by sender, topic, message length, and time of posting. The screened-out messages are not downloaded to your computer, and they do not appear on your message list.

Filter messages

In this exercise, you filter messages received from your news server.

1 On the Tools menu, click Newsgroup Filters.

The Newsgroup Filters dialog box appears.

2 In the Newsgroup Filters dialog box, click Add.

All Servers (All Files) is displayed in the Group(s) box. The rules you are setting up will apply to all files on all news servers.

3 In the Do Not Show Messages That Meet The Following Criteria area, in the Subject box, type **Cash**

People who post "get rich quick" messages often use the word "cash" in the subject to attract attention.

4 In the Do Not Show Messages That Meet The Following Criteria area, select the Messages Posted More Than check box, and then click the up arrow until the number reaches 3.

5 In the Properties dialog box, click OK.

The description of your newsgroup filter is displayed.

6 In the Newsgroup Filters dialog box, click OK.

The rules will be applied the next time you receive newsgroup messages.

Posting Messages

After you've read the FAQ and visited a newsgroup for a few days, you might want to start contributing to the newsgroup. You can contribute by posting replies to messages or by posting a new message and starting a new message thread. If someone is asking for help with a problem, it is common to send your reply only to the author of the message.

Internet Etiquette

Internet etiquette, or "netiquette," is an informal code of conduct that users of the Internet are expected to follow. You wouldn't send a disparaging message to someone in e-mail, and the same rule applies when you communicate in newsgroups. Beyond the warning to "be polite," there are some specific conventions you should keep in mind when you post messages to newsgroups. The following table describes some of these.

Things to remember	Why
Don't type in uppercase letters.	Uppercase text is considered SHOUTING, and readers don't want to be yelled at when they read newsgroup messages.
Be concise.	Try to state your point quickly. Many readers don't scroll through a message past the text in the preview pane.
Don't post meaningless messages.	If you want to post an "I agree" reply, you should also add something new to the discussion.
Be aware that your message could be misinterpreted.	Irony, sarcasm, and humor are hard to convey in print. You can use emoticons to help define your intentions, but your message might be misconstrued.
Get familiar with the newsgroup before you post messages.	Regular readers of the newsgroup don't want to see a new post about a topic that was covered the week before. Many newsgroups have an archive that you can search to see what topics have been discussed recently.

Reply to the newsgroup

Each newsgroup server has a test area where beginners can practice posting and replying to messages. To find your test area, you can generally type "beginner" or "test" in the Display Newsgroups Which Contain area of the Newsgroups dialog box. In this exercise, you reply to a message in the newsgroup.

1 On the toolbar, click Newsgroups.

2 In the Display Newsgroups Which Contain box, type **test**, but do not press ENTER.

A list of newsgroups with the word "test" in the name is displayed.

3 In the Newsgroups box, click a test newsgroup, and then click Go To.

The messages in the test newsgroup are displayed.

4 In the message list, click a message.

The message is displayed in the preview pane.

5 On the toolbar, click Reply To Group.

A new window opens. The original message is quoted below the insertion point with each line marked by a ">" symbol.

You can also click Reply To Newsgroup on the Compose menu.

6 At the insertion point, type **This is a test response. Please ignore.**

7 On the toolbar, click the Post Message button.

The Post News dialog box appears. You might get a message stating that not everyone can read HTML documents.

Post Message

8 In the Post News dialog box, select the Don't Show Me This Message Again check box, and click OK.

The message is posted to the newsgroup. You will not see it posted immediately, but you can return to this newsgroup at a later time to see the message.

Reply to the author only

In this exercise, you send a reply message to the author of the message only. The reply will be sent to the author's e-mail address.

You can also click Reply To Author on the Compose menu.

1 In the message list, click another message.

2 On the toolbar, click Reply To Author.

A new window opens.

3 At the insertion point, type **This is a test reply. Please ignore.**

4 On the toolbar, click Send.

The message is sent to the author's e-mail address.

Send

Post a new message to the newsgroup

In this exercise, you post a new message to the test newsgroup.

1 On the toolbar, click Compose Message.

A new window opens.

2 In the Subject box, type **This is a test.**

3 In the Message area, type **Test message. Please ignore.**

4 On the toolbar, click Post Message.

The message is posted to the newsgroup.

5 On the Outlook Bar, click the News Server icon.

NOTE If you'd like to build on the skills that you learned in this lesson, you can work through the exercises in One Step Further. Otherwise, skip to "Finish the lesson."

One Step Further: Cleaning Up Newsgroup Message Files

All the messages you read are stored in newsgroup message files. Your message files are refilled with messages from your news server each time you access a newsgroup. You should periodically clean up your files to conserve disk space and refresh the files. You can compact the files to regain wasted space, keep just the message headers, or delete all stored messages.

Compact the newsgroups

In this exercise, you compact a newsgroup to recover wasted space.

1 On the Tools menu, click Options.
2 In the Options dialog box, click the Advanced tab.
3 In the Local Message Files area, click Clean Up Now.

   The Local File Clean Up dialog box appears. The numbers in the File Information area tell you how much disk space your messages are using and how much wasted space will be recovered if you compact the files.
4 In the Local File(s) For box, be sure that All Servers (All Files) is displayed.

 TIP This setting indicates you are cleaning up all files. If you want to clean up only one newsgroup, you can click the Local File(s) For down arrow, and then select the newsgroup.

5 In the Local File Clean Up dialog box, click Delete.
6 In the Outlook Express dialog box, click Yes to confirm the deletion.

   The numbers in the File Information area show that your message files are empty.
7 In the Local File Clean Up dialog box, click Close.
8 In the Options dialog box, click OK.

If you are using a network connection, skip step 1.

Finish the lesson

Hang Up

1 On the toolbar, click Hang Up.
2 On the File menu, click Exit.

Lesson Summary

To	Do this	Button
Subscribe to a newsgroup	In the Newsgroups dialog box, click the newsgroup to which you want to subscribe, and then click Subscribe.	
Subscribe to a newsgroup while you are reading it	In the Folder list, select the newsgroup you want to read, and then click Go To. On the Tools menu, click Subscribe To This Group.	News groups
Read messages in the preview pane	In the message list, click the message you want to read.	
Read messages in a new window	In the message list, double-click the message you want to read.	
Read messages in a thread	In the message list, click the Plus icon to expand the thread. In the message list, click the message you want to read. To collapse the thread, in the message list, click the Minus icon.	
Mark a newsgroup for offline reading	On the newsgroups list, click the newsgroup you want to read offline. On the File menu, click Properties. Click the Download tab. Select the When Downloading This Newsgroup, Retrieve check box and the All Messages (Headers And Bodies) check box, and click OK.	
Download newsgroups for offline reading	On the Tools menu, click Download All.	
Read messages offline	In the list of newsgroups, click the newsgroup you want to read. In the message list, click the message you want to read.	
Print a message	In the list of newsgroups, click a newsgroup. Click the message you want to print. On the File menu, click Print. Click OK.	

141

To	Do this	Button
Save a message to disk	In the list of newsgroups. click a newsgroup. Click the message you want to save. On the File menu, click Save As. Click Save.	
Filter newsgroup messages	On the Tools menu, click Newsgroup Filters. Click Add. In the Subject box, type the word you want to screen out. Select the Messages Posted More Than check box. Click the up arrow until the number you want is displayed. Click OK until all dialog boxes are closed.	Reply to Group
Reply to the newsgroup	Select a newsgroup message. On the toolbar, click Reply To Group. At the insertion point, type your message. On the toolbar, click Post Message.	
Reply to the author only	Select a newsgroup message. On the toolbar, click Reply To Author. At the insertion point, type your message. On the toolbar, click Send.	Reply to Author
Post a new message to the newsgroup	On the toolbar, click Compose Message. In the Subject box, type the subject of the message. In the Message area, type your message. On the toolbar, click Post Message.	Compose Message

For online information about	**On the Help menu, click Contents And Index, click the Index tab, and then type**
Subscribing to newsgroups	**subscribing to newsgroups**
Reading newsgroup messages	**newsgroup messages**
Replying to newsgroup messages	**replying to newsgroup messages**
Posting a new message	**posting newsgroup messages**

Conducting Meetings on the Internet

In this lesson you will learn how to:

Estimated time
40 min.

- Contact other meeting participants.
- Hold a conversation with a meeting participant.
- Send and receive text messages in the Chat window.
- Use the Whiteboard to draw illustrations during a meeting.
- Collaborate on a document with another participant during a meeting.

Conducting a meeting online in NetMeeting is like holding a meeting in your conference room, except with NetMeeting you don't have to provide refreshments. In NetMeeting, you greet participants as they arrive, distribute handouts, and draw diagrams on the Whiteboard just as you would if all participants were in the same room.

NetMeeting is a multimedia program. If you and the other participants have microphones and speakers installed on your computers, you can talk to each other with NetMeeting. And, if you have cameras installed on your computers, you can meet face-to-face. Even without a camera, you can still receive video on the NetMeeting screen.

Although face-to-face or voice-to-voice contact is limited to two people at a time, everyone can contribute to the discussion by typing text messages in a Chat window. In addition, if you want to create a drawing during a meeting to make your point, you can do so on the Whiteboard; other participants can add to your drawing.

NetMeeting is ideal for conducting business meetings among people in different locations, and it is also great for communicating with friends whom you might not otherwise see very often.

 IMPORTANT   Speaking of friends, to learn how to use NetMeeting, you might want to contact a co-worker or friend who has also installed NetMeeting, and ask him or her to complete the exercises with you. If a co-worker or friend is not available, you can still complete the exercises if you don't mind talking to strangers who are also logged on to the NetMeeting server.

In your role as personnel director at Wide World Importers, you must discuss and distribute Personnel Policies and Procedures to the personnel managers in each region. You decide that instead of traveling to each site, you will conduct a meeting online using Microsoft NetMeeting. You enlist a co-worker to help you learn how to use NetMeeting.

Start NetMeeting

In this exercise, you start NetMeeting from the Desktop.

 IMPORTANT   You must have NetMeeting set up to complete this lesson. For more information, see the "Setting Up NetMeeting" section of Appendix A.

You can also start NetMeeting from Internet Explorer or from Outlook Express by clicking Internet Call on the Go menu.

If you are using a network connection, skip step 2.

1   On the taskbar, click Start, point to Programs, Internet Explorer and then click NetMeeting.

The NetMeeting program starts.

2   In the Password box, type your password.

The Microsoft NetMeeting window opens. If you are using MSN, you are logged on to the default server, and a directory of the other people who are logged on to the server is displayed on the Directory screen. Your screen should look similar to the following illustration.

On a call   Has video capabilities

Directory list

Has audio capabilities

Calling Other Participants

Calling people in NetMeeting is like calling people on the telephone, except that you can include more than one person in the call. Suppose you have four people that you want to include in a meeting. You schedule a meeting time, and each person logs on to the NetMeeting server at that time. You see the names of the other people on the directory list, so you call each one. When each person accepts your call, your meeting is formed, and you can open the Chat window and start the discussion.

You can save or print all the messages displayed in the Chat window. Saving a record of the meeting is useful if you need to produce minutes for the meeting. You can save the file to disk and edit it later. If you need a printout of the discussion, you can print from the Chat window.

The e-mail addresses of people who you call and people who call you are added automatically to your Speed Dial list. (This option is located on the Tools menu, in the Options dialog box Calling tab, and you can change it if you want.) Speed Dial is handy because it saves you the trouble of looking for names in the directory list.

During the meeting, if you want to speak to another person or meet face-to-face, you can select that person's name from a list. This establishes an audio and video connection between you and that person. You can make this connection with either audio or video; you do not have to have access to both. When you are finished talking to that person, you can switch the connection and talk to another person in the meeting.

If you do not want to be interrupted with other calls during a meeting, you can put out a Do Not Disturb sign by clicking Do Not Disturb on the Call menu.

Review the calling options

Before you place a call, you should review the calling options controlling how your calls are placed and received in NetMeeting. When you log on to the server, your name is displayed on the directory list, and others who are logged on to the server can call you. You want to set your calling options so that you have the choice of accepting or ignoring an incoming call. You also need to set your audio options so that you can send and receive audio without stopping the conversation. In this exercise, you review your calling options to make sure that you do not accept calls automatically, and set up your audio options for voice transmissions.

1   On the Tools menu, click Options.

2   On the General tab, be sure that the Automatically Accept Incoming Calls check box is not selected.

    By not selecting this option, you will be asked if you want to accept a call when someone calls you.

3   In the Options dialog box, click the Audio tab.

4   In the General area, select the Enable Full Duplex Audio So I Can Speak While Receiving Audio check box.

    Full duplex audio allows you and the other person to speak at the same time without pausing. To use full duplex audio, you must have a full-duplex sound card installed on your PC. If you have a half-duplex sound card, you will have to pause after you are finished speaking or say something like "over" when you are finished.

5   In the Options dialog box, click OK.

Place a call

If more than one person is scheduled to attend the meeting, you can call each person or wait until they call you. In this exercise, you call your co-worker from the directory list.

IMPORTANT Your co-worker must be using NetMeeting and must be logged on to the same server you are on for the call to be completed.

1   On the Directory list, scroll down until you locate the name of your co-worker, and then click the name.

2   On the toolbar, click Call.

    The New Call dialog box appears.

Call

You can also click New Call on the Call menu.

3   In the New Call dialog box, click Call.

TIP When you place a call, the address you are calling is saved in your Speed Dial area. The next time you want to call that person, you can call quickly using Speed Dial.

The call is placed. On the receiving end, a dialog box appears to notify your co-worker that you are calling. When you receive a call, you have the choice of accepting the call or ignoring it. Your co-worker should click the Accept button to accept the call. When the call is accepted, your screen changes from the directory list to the Current Call screen.

Talk to a meeting participant

In this exercise, you talk to your co-worker using NetMeeting and adjust your microphone and speaker volume while you are talking.

1   To talk to your co-worker, speak into your microphone.

    On the toolbar, you can drag the Audio slider to adjust the microphone.

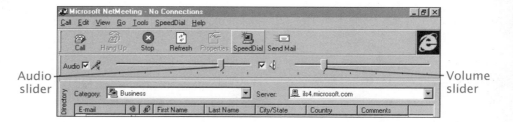

2   Ask your co-worker to speak into the microphone.

    On the toolbar, you can use the Volume slider to adjust your speaker volume.

147

Talking to Other Meeting Participants

When you have finished a conversation with one person, you can switch the audio and video connections and talk to someone else in the meeting.

Switch the connection

In this exercise, you switch the connection.

1 On the toolbar, click Switch.

   A list of the people in the meeting is displayed with a check mark next to the person with the current connection.

2 Click the name that is checked.

   A dialog box appears to be sure that you want to stop the connection.

3 In the dialog box, check the Don't Show Me This Message Again check box, and click OK.

   The check mark is removed from the name.

4 On the toolbar, click Switch, and then click another name.

   You can also right-click the name in the Current Call screen to stop or start a connection.

Distribute handouts

If you are meeting in a conference room, you generally distribute handouts or an agenda to the meeting participants as they walk in the door. You can also distribute handouts in NetMeeting by sending a file containing the handouts to participants. In this exercise, you send a file containing the meeting agenda to your co-worker.

IMPORTANT To complete this lesson, you must have the practice files installed. For more information, see the "Installing and Using Practice Files" section at the front of this book.

1 In the Current Call screen, right-click your co-worker's name.

   A shortcut menu is displayed.

2 On the shortcut menu, click Send File.

3 In the Select A File To Send dialog box, click the Look In down arrow, and then select the folder where the Policy.doc practice file is stored.

4 Click the Policy.doc file, and then click Send.

The file is sent in the background. You can continue your conversation as the file is transmitted. A dialog box appears to inform you that the file was sent successfully.

5 When the transmission is complete, in the Microsoft NetMeeting dialog box, click OK.

A Transfer dialog box appears for your co-worker. For your co-worker to view the file, he or she can click the Open button in the Transfer dialog box.

Sending and Receiving Messages

In NetMeeting, you can send and receive messages through a Chat window or via the audio and video connections. Both methods have their advantages. With a Chat window, you can save or print a record of the meeting. With the audio and video connections, you can explain concepts that might be difficult to express in writing. NetMeeting allows you to select the type of communication that is most appropriate for each meeting, including the option of using both methods during a single meeting.

Sending and Receiving Messages in the Chat Window

If you have several people in a meeting, you can use the Chat window to enable everyone to participate in the discussion. All participants see messages in the Chat window as the messages are entered. When one person opens a Chat window, the window opens automatically on everyone else's NetMeeting screen.

Send and receive messages in the Chat window

In this exercise, you use the Chat window to send and receive messages.

Chat

1 On the toolbar, click Chat.

A Chat window opens.

2 In the Send To box, be sure that Everyone In Chat is selected.

This setting ensures that everyone in the meeting can contribute to the discussion.

 TIP If you want to send a private message to one participant, you can click the Send To down arrow and then select the participant's name. The notation "private" is automatically added to the message.

---

3 In the Message box, type **Welcome to the meeting.** and press ENTER.

The message is displayed in your co-worker's Chat window.

You can still speak into the microphone when you are in the Chat window.

4 Ask your co-worker to type **It's nice to be here.** and press ENTER.

When your co-worker enters a message, it is displayed in your Chat window. The author of the message is listed in the left column, with the text of the message shown in the right column. Your screen should look similar to the following illustration.

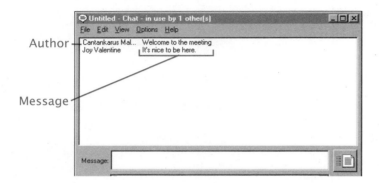

Change the Chat format

You can change the appearance of messages on your Chat screen. In this exercise, you add the date and time to your Chat messages.

1 On the Options menu, click Chat Format.

2 In the Chat Format dialog box, in the Information Display area, select the Date check box and the Time check box, and click OK.

The date and time are added to the messages on your screen only. Resetting the chat format does not affect the screen display for your co-worker.

Print your chat

In this exercise, you print the chat messages to keep a record of the discussion.

1 On the File menu, click Print.

The Print dialog box appears.

2 In the Copies area, click the up arrow until the number reaches 2.

You can print a copy for you and your co-worker.

3 In the Print dialog box, click OK.

The chat messages are printed.

Save your chat

When you close the Chat window, the message text is cleared. Chat messages are not saved unless you save them to a file on disk. Saving the messages to a file is helpful if you are recording the minutes of a meeting and need the messages in electronic format so they can be edited later. In this exercise, you save your Chat messages.

1 In the Chat window, on the File menu, click Save.

   The Save As dialog box appears.

2 In the File Name box, type Chat, and then click Save.

   The file is saved in the location indicated in the Save In box

3 Close the Chat window.

   The Chat window closes, and the Current Call window opens.

Drawing on the Whiteboard

You can use the Whiteboard in NetMeeting the same way you use a whiteboard in a conference room. All participants in the meeting see the drawing instantly and unless you lock the Whiteboard, everyone can contribute to the drawing.

You can use multiple pages on the Whiteboard if you need more drawing space or if you want to simulate a flip chart.

Create and edit a drawing

In this exercise, you draw an organization chart on the Whiteboard.

Whiteboard

1 On the toolbar, click Whiteboard.

   The Whiteboard program opens on your computer and on your co-worker's computer. If you have used other draw programs, such as Microsoft Paint, the toolbars and commands will be familiar to you.

Unfilled Rectangle

2 On the toolbar, click the Unfilled Rectangle button.

3 On the Whiteboard, draw three rectangles to illustrate an organization chart.

   Your co-worker sees the rectangles as you draw them, and if your co-worker draws on the Whiteboard, you will see your co-worker's graphics added to your drawing.

Text

4 On the toolbar, click the Text button.

5 To complete the graphic, in the three rectangles, type **Personnel**, **Manufacturing**, and **Sales** (in this order).

Insert New Page

Previous

6 In the lower-right corner of the toolbar, click the Insert New Page button.

The current page is moved to page 2, and a new, blank page is displayed on the Whiteboard.

7 On the toolbar, click the Previous page button.

Your three-rectangle diagram is displayed .

Lock the Whiteboard

In this exercise, you lock the Whiteboard so that you are the only participant who can draw on it.

Lock Contents

1 On the toolbar, click the Lock Contents button.

A padlock icon is displayed on your co-worker's screen, and all of your co-worker's drawing tools become unavailable for use. Your co-worker cannot draw on the Whiteboard while you have it locked. The same button is used to lock and unlock the Whiteboard.

Unlock Contents

2 To unlock the Whiteboard, click the Unlock Contents button again.

The Whiteboard is open to all participants.

Print the Whiteboard

In this exercise, you print the drawing on the Whiteboard.

IMPORTANT To complete this exercise, you must have a printer available from your computer.

1 On the File menu, click Print.

The Print dialog box appears.

2 In the Print Range area, select the All check box, and click OK.

The drawing is printed.

Save the Whiteboard

You can use a drawing you create on the Whiteboard in another NetMeeting session. In this exercise, you save the drawing on the Whiteboard to a file on disk.

1 On the File menu, click Save.

NOTE If you have saved the file before, the Save option automatically saves the file under the current file name. To save the file under a new name, on the File menu, click Save As.

2 In the File Name box, type **orgchart**, and then click Save.

The file is saved in the location shown in the Save In box under the file name orgchart.wht.

3 Close the Whiteboard.

Collaborating on Documents

Co-authoring a document can be time-consuming if you are sending printouts or files back and forth. In NetMeeting, you can collaborate on a document online and get instant feedback as changes are made in the document.

Collaborating on a document means that you are sharing the document in its original program with other people in NetMeeting. Up to three participants can collaborate on a document, even if the original program is not on every participant's computer.

When collaborating on a document in NetMeeting, each collaborator takes turns. One person has control of the document and can make changes to it before handing it off to another participant. When you collaborate, you are sharing the document's original program with your collaborators.

Share a program

In this exercise, you open the FrontPage Express program so you and your co-worker can collaborate on a Web page.

IMPORTANT To complete this exercise, you will need to have the practice files installed. For more information, see the "Installing and Using the Practice Files" section at the front of this book.

Open

Share

You can also point to Share Application on the Tools menu, and then click FrontPage Express.

1 On the taskbar, click Start, point to Programs, point to Internet Explorer, and then click FrontPage Express.

You must have the original program open to collaborate on the document.

2 In the FrontPage Express window, on the toolbar, click the Open button.

3 In the From File area, click Browse. Click the Look In down arrow and select Internet Explorer 4 SBS Practice.

4 In the Open File dialog box, click the Pers.htm file, and then click Open.

5 On the taskbar, click Microsoft NetMeeting.

The NetMeeting window opens.

6 On the toolbar, click Share, and then click FrontPage Express.

A dialog box to confirm the action appears.

7 In the Microsoft NetMeeting dialog box, click OK.

Collaborate on a document

In this exercise, you collaborate on a document in FrontPage Express.

Collaborate

You can still speak into the microphone while you are collaborating.

1 On the toolbar, click Collaborate.

A message warning you that collaborating makes your files available to others is displayed.

2 In the Microsoft NetMeeting dialog box, click OK. On the taskbar, click FrontPage.

By viewing the Sharing column, you can tell who is in control of the document. Only one person can be in control at a time.

3 Ask your co-worker to double-click any blank area in the FrontPage Express window.

The document is displayed, and your co-worker has control of the file. When your co-worker has control, you cannot move your mouse pointer. The person in control of the file can edit the file. Changes that are entered are displayed simultaneously on both screens.

4 In the Current Call window, click any blank area to regain control of the file.

5 When you are finished, on the toolbar, click Collaborate.

Your co-worker will also need to click the Collaborate button to stop collaborating.

The Collaborate button is a toggle that turns collaboration on and off. A dialog box explaining that control will be returned to you appears.

6 In the Microsoft NetMeeting dialog box, and click OK.

7 On the taskbar, click FrontPage Express.

8 Close the FrontPage Express window.

Ending a Call

When you are finished with a call, you can hang up and either stay connected to the NetMeeting server to call someone else or exit NetMeeting.

End a call

In this exercise, you hang up your NetMeeting call.

Hang Up

You can also click Hang Up on the Call menu.

 On the toolbar, click Hang Up.

The call is ended. You are still connected to the server and you can place other calls.

 TIP If you want to remove one person from the meeting, in the Current Call area, right-click the name, and then click Remove From Meeting.

154

Exit NetMeeting

In this exercise, you log off the ils.microsoft.com server and exit NetMeeting.

1   On the Call menu, click Log Off From.

A dialog box confirming that you want to log off the server appears.

2   In the dialog box, select the Don't Show Me This Message Again check box, and click OK.

You are logged off the server, and your status is indicated on the status bar.

3   On the Call menu, click Exit.

The NetMeeting program closes, and the Connection dialog box appears.

4   In the Connected dialog box, click Yes.

You are still connected to the Internet.

NOTE   If you'd like to build on the skills that you learned in this lesson, you can work through the exercises in One Step Further. Otherwise, skip to "Finish the lesson."

One Step Further: Viewing a Multimedia Presentation

In addition to NetMeeting, there is another program available with Internet Explorer that uses multimedia. NetShow displays audio and video presentations on your computer. You can use NetShow to create and distribute training videos in your company or to make a personal video available to family and friends on your personal Web page. You can view a NetShow presentation from within Internet Explorer, or you can access the NetShow Player directly from the Internet Explorer menu.

View a NetShow presentation

In this exercise, you view a NetShow presentation from the Microsoft NetShow Web page.

1   On the taskbar, click the Launch Internet Explorer icon.

The Internet Explorer window opens.

2   In the Address bar, type **www.microsoft.com/netshow/samples.htm** and press ENTER.

The NetShow Gallery page appears. You do not need to load the NetShow Player; it is included in the full installation of Internet Explorer.

3   On the Gallery page, click the Samples tab.

4   On the Samples page, click Directions From SeaTac To Microsoft.

 NOTE   If the Directions From SeaTac To Microsoft link is not listed, select a different link.

The NetShow Player window opens, and the multimedia presentation is displayed in the NetShow Player. You can track the progress of the presentation on the slider bar. Your screen should look similar to the following illustration.

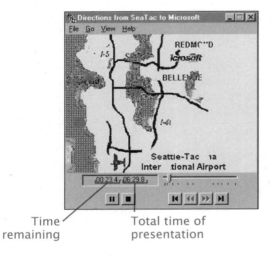

Time remaining   Total time of presentation

5   When the presentation is finished, close the NetPlayer window.

6   Close the Internet Explorer window.

Finish the lesson

If you are using a network connection, skip this exercise.

▶   On the taskbar, right-click the Dial-Up Connection icon, and then click Disconnect.

Lesson Summary

To	Do this	Button
Change your calling options	On the Tools menu, click Options. On the General tab, be sure that Automatically Accept Incoming Calls is not selected. Click the Audio tab, and than select the Enable Full Duplex Audio So I Can Speak While Receiving Audio check box. In the Options dialog box, click OK.	
Place a call	On the Directory list, click the person you want to call. On the toolbar, click Call. In the New Call dialog box, click Call.	
Talk to a meeting participant and adjust audio	Speak into the microphone. Move the Audio and Volume slider bars to adjust the sound.	
Send a file to participants	In the Current Call screen, right-click the participant's name. On the shortcut menu, click Send File. In the Select A File To Send dialog box, select the file you want to send, and then click Send. In the dialog box, to confirm that you want to send the file, click OK.	
Send and receive messages in the Chat window	On the toolbar, click Chat. In the Send To box, be sure that Everyone In Chat is selected. In the Message box, type your message, and press ENTER.	
Change the format of a Chat message	In the Chat window, on the Options menu, click Chat Format. In the Information Display area, select the Date check box and the Time check box, and click OK.	
Print your chat	In the Chat window, on the File menu, click Print. In the Print dialog box, click OK.	

To	Do this	Button
Save your chat	In the Chat window, on the File menu, click Save. In the File Name box, type the name of the file, and then click Save. Close the Chat window.	
Draw on the Whiteboard	On the toolbar, click Whiteboard. In the Whiteboard window, on the toolbar, select the Unfilled Rectangle button. On the Whiteboard, draw a rectangle. On the toolbar, select the Text button, and then type text in the rectangle.	
Lock and unlock the Whiteboard	On the toolbar, click the Lock Contents button.	
Print the Whiteboard	In the Whiteboard window, on the File menu, click Print. In the Print Range area, select the All check box, and click OK.	
Share a program	On the taskbar, click Start, point to Programs, select the program you want to share. On the toolbar, click Open. In the From File area, click Browse. In the Open File dialog box, click the file you want to open, and then click Open. On the taskbar, click Microsoft NetMeeting. On the toolbar, click Share, and then click FrontPage Express. In the dialog box, click OK.	

To	Do this	Button
Collaborate on a document	On the toolbar, click Collaborate. In the dialog box, click OK. Ask your co-worker to double-click any blank area. In the Current Call window, click any blank area to retain control of the document. When you are finished, on the toolbar, click Collaborate. On the taskbar, click FrontPage Express. In the FrontPage Express window, on the File menu, click Save. In the Save Changes dialog box, click Yes. Close the FrontPage Express window.	
End a call	On the toolbar, click Hang Up.	
Disconnect from the server and exit NetMeeting	On the Call menu, click Log Off From ils.microsoft.com. On the Call menu, click Exit.	

For online information about	On the Help menu, click Contents And Index, click the Index tab, and then type
Calling meeting participants	**placing a call**
Talking to other participants	**talking over the Internet**
Using the Chat window to communicate	**Chat**
Drawing on the Whiteboard	**Whiteboard**
Collaborating on a document	**collaborating**

Review & Practice

Estimated time
25 min.

You will review and practice how to:

■ Create and send an e-mail message.
■ Reply to an e-mail message.
■ Subscribe to a newsgroup.
■ Post a newsgroup message.
■ Meet with people over the Internet.

Before you complete this book, you can practice the skills you learned in Part 3 by working through this Review & Practice section. You will compose and send an e-mail message and reply to the message. You will also subscribe to a newsgroup, post a new message to a newsgroup, and meet with another person using the Microsoft NetMeeting program.

Scenario

In your role as accounting manager at Wide World Importers, you have implemented a company-wide upgrade to all accounting systems. You are considering writing an article for a trade publication on how the upgrade was accomplished. You want to collaborate on the article with the training manager, who is based in Atlanta (you are in Seattle).

Step 1: *Create and Send an E-mail Message*

You send an e-mail message to the training manager in the Atlanta office to see if the manager wants to collaborate on an article about your recent accounting systems upgrade.

1 Start Outlook Express.

2 Create a new e-mail message, and address it to your e-mail address. Type **Collaboration** as the subject of the message.

 NOTE Normally, you would not send a message to yourself. However, in this Review & Practice you will send a message to your e-mail address, and then respond to the message.

3 Type the following text as the message text.

Would you like to collaborate on an article for The Accountant's Journal?

4 Send the message.

For more information about	See
Composing e-mail messages	Lesson 6
Sending e-mail messages	Lesson 6

Step 2: *Reply to an E-mail Message*

In this step, you reply to the Collaboration message and print the message.

1 Receive your new mail.

2 Open the Collaboration message. (Hint: The message is in your Inbox.)

3 Type the following text as the reply text.

A collaboration sounds interesting. I'll start gathering information.

4 Send the reply.

5 Print the reply message.

For more information about	See
Receiving new mail	Lesson 6
Replying to a message	Lesson 6
Printing messages	Lesson 6

Step 3: *Subscribe to a Newsgroup*

You decide to subscribe to a business newsgroup to see if there are any discussions about accounting systems similar to yours.

1 Access your news server's list of newsgroups. (Hint: Your news server's icon is on the Outlook Bar.)

2 Search for newsgroups with "biz.comp" in the name.

3 Subscribe to the biz.comp.accounting newsgroup.

 NOTE If the biz.comp.accounting newsgroup is not on your list, subscribe to a different newsgroup.

4 Read the messages in the biz.comp.accounting newsgroup.

For more information about	See
Searching for newsgroups	Lesson 7
Subscribing to newsgroups	Lesson 7
Reading newsgroup messages	Lesson 7

Step 4: *Post a Newsgroup Message*

You post a new message to a newsgroup, requesting people who are interested in contributing to your article to contact you at your e-mail address.

 NOTE In this step, you will post a message to the alt.test newsgroup. Since this message will be posted on the Internet, you will use a test message. If you send a message asking for people who want to contribute to an article, don't be surprised if you get some replies!

1 Go to the alt.test newsgroup.

2 Compose a new message, and type **Test** as the subject.

3 Type the following text as the message text.

  This is a test message.

4 Post the message.

5 Hang up your Internet connection, and exit Outlook Express.

For more information about	See
Searching for newsgroups	Lesson 7
Posting a new message to a newsgroup	Lesson 7

Step 5:   *Meet with People on the Internet*

Your deadline is just a few weeks away, so you meet online with the training manager to develop the outline for the article.

 IMPORTANT   To complete this step, you will need to ask a co-worker or friend to start NetMeeting and log on to the ils.microsoft.com server.

1   Start NetMeeting.

2   In NetMeeting, call your co-worker or friend.

3   Open the Notepad text editor. (Hint: On the Start menu, point to Accessories, and then click Notepad.)

4   Type **I. Overview**, and press ENTER.

5   Ask your co-worker or friend to take control of the file, and type **A. Getting Started**.

6   Regain control of the file.

7   Stop collaborating.

8   Save the file as Outline.txt, and exit Notepad. (Make a note of where the file is stored. You will need to delete it later in the "Finish the lesson" exercise.)

9   Hang up the call, and log off the server.

10   Exit NetMeeting, and disconnect from the Internet.

For more information about	See
Starting NetMeeting	Lesson 8
Placing a call	Lesson 8
Sharing a program	Lesson 8
Collaborating on a document	Lesson 8
Ending a call	Lesson 8
Exiting NetMeeting	Lesson 8

Finish the Review & Practice

Follow these steps to delete the practice messages and the outline you created in this Review & Practice.

1   In Outlook Express, delete all files in your Inbox and your Sent Items folder.

2   Exit Outlook Express.

3   On the Desktop, open My Computer, and locate the Outline.txt file.

4   Delete the Outline.txt file.

5   Close all open windows on the Desktop.

Index

A

Active Desktop. *See also* Desktop
  adding items, 57–58
  defined, 55
  displaying Web pages, 59–60
  Gallery, 57–58
Address bar
  adding to taskbar, 60
  and Autosearch, 24
  defined, 37
  entering URLs, 8–9
addresses
  adding to Wallet, 15
  creating groups, 116–17
  for e-mail messages, 105, 115–17, 118
  finding, 118
  World Wide Web syntax, 7–8
Alternative (alt) Usenet category, 127
applications, sharing in NetMeeting, 153–54
articles, newsgroup. *See* messages, newsgroup
attached files, 110, 113
AutoComplete, 9
Autosearch, 24

B

Back button, 10
backgrounds, saving, 85
Book Radio, 56
browsers, defined, 4. *See also* Internet Explorer
browsing Web pages, 4, 7–10
Business (biz) Usenet category, 127
business meetings, online. *See* NetMeeting

C

calculator site, 28
calling NetMeeting participants, 145–48
CC messages, 107
Center for Democracy and Privacy, 44
Channel Bar, 55, 62–64, 67
Channel Definition Format (CDF), 62
Channel Guide, 62–64
channels
  adding subscriptions, 61, 62–64
  defined, 55–56
  updating subscriptions manually, 65–66
  vs. Favorites list, 61
Channel Viewer, 69

Chat window
  defined, 149
  printing chat, 150
  saving NetMeeting chat, 151
  using in NetMeeting, 149–50
collaborating, on NetMeeting documents, 153–54
colors, overriding default colors for Web links, 35–36
composing e-mail messages, 105–8, 110–11
Computer Network, 19
Computers (comp) Usenet category, 127
com sites, 8
content
  defined, 11
  providers, 11, 12–13, 21
  ratings guide, 13–14
  subscribing to, 61
conversation, real-time, 147–48, 149–50
cookies, 44, 45
copyright, 84
country codes, 8
crawlers, 23
credit cards, 15–16

D

Daily schedule, 69–71
Deja News, 126
Deleted Items folder, 105
Desktop
  accessing Favorites list, 30
  Active Desktop, 55, 57–60
  adding Address bar, 60
  adding Investor Ticker, 57–58
  adding Web to, 57–60
  creating Internet shortcuts on, 10–11
  displaying Web pages on, 59–60
  downloading Microsoft Daily News to, 59–60
DESKTOP.INI file, 93
dial-up connections, 4. *See also* Microsoft Network, The
digital signatures, 109
documents, collaborating on, 153–54
domain names, 7–8
downloading. *See also* subscriptions
  hiding dialog box, 66
  Investor Ticker, 57–58
  Microsoft Daily News, 59–60
  newsgroups, 133–34

167

Index

IMPORTANT—READ CAREFULLY BEFORE OPENING SOFTWARE PACKET(S). By opening the sealed packet(s) containing the software, you indicate your acceptance of the following Microsoft License Agreement.

MICROSOFT LICENSE AGREEMENT

(Book Companion CD)

This is a legal agreement between you (either an individual or an entity) and Microsoft Corporation. By opening the sealed software packet(s) you are agreeing to be bound by the terms of this agreement. If you do not agree to the terms of this agreement, promptly return the unopened software packet(s) and any accompanying written materials to the place you obtained them for a full refund.

MICROSOFT SOFTWARE LICENSE

1. GRANT OF LICENSE. Microsoft grants to you the right to use one copy of the Microsoft software program included with this book (the "SOFTWARE") on a single terminal connected to a single computer. The SOFTWARE is in "use" on a computer when it is loaded into the temporary memory (i.e., RAM) or installed into the permanent memory (e.g., hard disk, CD-ROM, or other storage device) of that computer. You may not network the SOFTWARE or otherwise use it on more than one computer or computer terminal at the same time. For the files and material referenced in this book which may be obtained from the Internet, Microsoft grants to you the right to use the materials in connection with the book. If you are a member of a corporation or business, you may reproduce the materials and distribute them within your business for internal business purposes in connection with the book. You may not reproduce the materials for further distribution.

2. COPYRIGHT. The SOFTWARE is owned by Microsoft or its suppliers and is protected by United States copyright laws and international treaty provisions. Therefore, you must treat the SOFTWARE like any other copyrighted material (e.g., a book or musical recording) except that you may either (a) make one copy of the SOFTWARE solely for backup or archival purposes, or (b) transfer the SOFTWARE to a single hard disk provided you keep the original solely for backup or archival purposes. You may not copy the written materials accompanying the SOFTWARE.

3. OTHER RESTRICTIONS. You may not rent or lease the SOFTWARE, but you may transfer the SOFTWARE and accompanying written materials on a permanent basis provided you retain no copies and the recipient agrees to the terms of this Agreement. You may not reverse engineer, decompile, or disassemble the SOFTWARE. If the SOFTWARE is an update or has been updated, any transfer must include the most recent update and all prior versions.

4. DUAL MEDIA SOFTWARE. If the SOFTWARE package contains more than one kind of disk (3.5", 5.25", and CD-ROM), then you may use only the disks appropriate for your single-user computer. You may not use the other disks on another computer or loan, rent, lease, or transfer them to another user except as part of the permanent transfer (as provided above) of all SOFTWARE and written materials.

5. SAMPLE CODE. If the SOFTWARE includes Sample Code, then Microsoft grants you a royalty-free right to reproduce and distribute the sample code of the SOFTWARE provided that you: (a) distribute the sample code only in conjunction with and as a part of your software product; (b) do not use Microsoft's or its authors' names, logos, or trademarks to market your software product; (c) include the copyright notice that appears on the SOFTWARE on your product label and as a part of the sign-on message for your software product; and (d) agree to indemnify, hold harmless, and defend Microsoft and its authors from and against any claims or lawsuits, including attorneys' fees, that arise or result from the use or distribution of your software product.

DISCLAIMER OF WARRANTY

The SOFTWARE (including instructions for its use) is provided "AS IS" WITHOUT WARRANTY OF ANY KIND. MICROSOFT FURTHER DISCLAIMS ALL IMPLIED WARRANTIES INCLUDING WITHOUT LIMITATION ANY IMPLIED WARRANTIES OF MERCHANTABILITY OR OF FITNESS FOR A PARTICULAR PURPOSE. THE ENTIRE RISK ARISING OUT OF THE USE OR PERFORMANCE OF THE SOFTWARE AND DOCUMENTATION REMAINS WITH YOU.

IN NO EVENT SHALL MICROSOFT, ITS AUTHORS, OR ANYONE ELSE INVOLVED IN THE CREATION, PRODUCTION, OR DELIVERY OF THE SOFTWARE BE LIABLE FOR ANY DAMAGES WHATSOEVER (INCLUDING, WITHOUT LIMITATION, DAMAGES FOR LOSS OF BUSINESS PROFITS, BUSINESS INTERRUPTION, LOSS OF BUSINESS INFORMATION, OR OTHER PECUNIARY LOSS) ARISING OUT OF THE USE OF OR INABILITY TO USE THE SOFTWARE OR DOCUMENTATION, EVEN IF MICROSOFT HAS BEEN ADVISED OF THE POSSIBILITY OF SUCH DAMAGES. BECAUSE SOME STATES/COUNTRIES DO NOT ALLOW THE EXCLUSION OR LIMITATION OF LIABILITY FOR CONSEQUENTIAL OR INCIDENTAL DAMAGES, THE ABOVE LIMITATION MAY NOT APPLY TO YOU.

U.S. GOVERNMENT RESTRICTED RIGHTS

The SOFTWARE and documentation are provided with RESTRICTED RIGHTS. Use, duplication, or disclosure by the Government is subject to restrictions as set forth in subparagraph (c)(1)(ii) of The Rights in Technical Data and Computer Software clause at DFARS 252.227-7013 or subparagraphs (c)(1) and (2) of the Commercial Computer Software — Restricted Rights 48 CFR 52.227-19, as applicable. Manufacturer is Microsoft Corporation, One Microsoft Way, Redmond, WA 98052-6399.

If you acquired this product in the United States, this Agreement is governed by the laws of the State of Washington.

Should you have any questions concerning this Agreement, or if you desire to contact Microsoft Press for any reason, please write: Microsoft Press, One Microsoft Way, Redmond, WA 98052-6399.

The
Microsoft®
Internet Explorer
Step by Step CD-ROM

The enclosed CD-ROM contains Internet Explorer 4; timesaving, ready-to-use practice files that complement the lessons in this book; and much more. To use the CD, you'll need either the Windows 95 operating system or the Windows NT version 4 operating system with Service Pack 3 or later installed.

Before you begin the Step by Step lessons, read the "Using the Microsoft Internet Explorer 4 Step by Step CD-ROM" section of this book. There you'll find detailed information about the contents of the CD and easy instructions telling how to install the files on your computer's hard disk.

Please take a few moments to read the License Agreement on the previous page before using the enclosed CD.

Register your Microsoft Press® book today, and let us know what you think.

At Microsoft Press, we listen to our customers. We update our books as new releases of software are issued, and we'd like you to tell us the kinds of additional information you'd find most useful in these updates. Your feedback will be considered when we prepare a future edition; plus, when you become a registered owner, you will get Microsoft Press catalogs and exclusive offers on specially priced books.

Thanks!

I used this book as
- ● A way to learn the software
- ● A reference when I needed it
- ● A way to find out about advanced features
- ● Other_____

I purchased this book from
- ● A bookstore
- ● A software store
- ● A direct mail offer
- ● Other_____

I consider myself
- ● A beginner or an occasional computer user
- ● An intermediate-level user with a pretty good grasp of the basics
- ● An advanced user who helps and provides solutions for others
- ● Other_____

I will buy the next edition of the book when it's updated
- ● Definitely
- ● Probably
- ● I will not buy the next edition

The next edition of this book should include the following additional information:

1•_____

2•_____

3•_____

The most useful things about this book are_____

_____

This book would be more helpful if_____

_____

My general impressions of this book are_____

_____

May we contact you regarding your comments?   ● Yes   ● No

Would you like to receive a Microsoft Press catalog regularly?   ● Yes   ● No

Name_____

Company (if applicable)_____

Address_____

City_____State_____Zip_____

Daytime phone number (optional) (_____)_____

Please mail back your feedback form—postage free! Fold this form as described on the other side of this card, or fax this sheet to:
Microsoft Press, Attn: Marketing Department, fax 425-936-7329

NO POSTAGE
NECESSARY
IF MAILED
IN THE
UNITED STATES

BUSINESS REPLY MAIL

FIRST-CLASS MAIL   PERMIT NO. 53   BOTHELL, WA

POSTAGE WILL BE PAID BY ADDRESSEE

MICROSOFT PRESS
MICROSOFT® INTERNET EXPLORER 4
STEP BY STEP
PO BOX 3019
BOTHELL WA   98041-9946